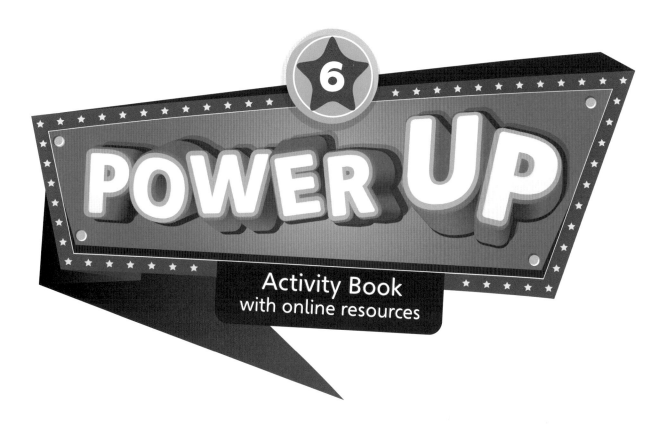

6

Power UP

Activity Book
with online resources

T0392213

Melanie Starren

With Caroline Nixon and Michael Tomlinson

Map of the book

A song and a dance

My goal

I can have a simple conversation about a familiar topic. **5**

Mission Complete!

I can write an email stating preferences and making suggestions. **4**

I can find specific information in simple texts. **3**

I can find out and write about the life of a popular musician. **2**

I can understand about music when I read a text. **1**

Diary

What I already know about music …

What I have learned about music …

And I need …

To do this, I will …

So I can …

I want to practise …

1 Make five music words using the music notes.

1 _____ 2 _____ 3 _____ 4 _____ 5 _____

2 🎧 4.02 Listen and read. Complete with the correct type of music.

opera   classical music   folk   music   disco

1

I went to a concert at the Royal Albert Hall in London during the holidays. I don't usually enjoy listening to _____ because my mum plays it ALL THE TIME at home and the concerts are all very long. But this was different. It was for kids and teenagers so it was more relaxed. This time the concert only lasted for an hour. I think I might go again. Do you fancy coming with me?

Kamile

2

My sister, Lucia, is really into music from the 60s and 70s. I was looking through her old vinyl records last week and found this one. I know you prefer hip-hop, and I do too, but I was actually pretty impressed with it. Listen first then tell me if _____ is for you!

Anna

3

I'm going to the Green Man festival in Wales next week. I can't wait! I like _____ music, there's so much at the Green Man festival for people our age! Even though I usually hate camping, the facilities here are great!

Jaime

3 Read the texts again. Say *yes* or *no*.

1 The concert at the Royal Albert Hall was too long.

2 Anna's song is different from the music she usually likes.

3 Jaime is sleeping in a tent.

4 Andrea is a fan of opera.

4

 ⭐⭐⭐⭐⭐ **ONLINE REVIEW**

A lot of people like _____ but I can't understand a single word they say! The women's voices are too high and the men's voices are far too low. I just want to understand the story! *Andrea*

1 ⭐ **For each question, choose the correct answer.**

1

Win a family ticket for the Madrid Jazz Festival. Tell us, in 50 words, why you want the tickets to this event. Note – the winner must have at least one person under 14 in their family.

What must you do in order to win the competition?

A write about why you would like to go to the festival

B write about why you have never been to the festival

C write about which family member you want to take to the festival

2

Hi Joe,

Did you see David Bisbal on TV last night? He did an interview and performed his latest song. It may be online if you missed it. I know you like him!

Claire

Why has Claire sent this text message?

A to tell Joe where he might possibly be able to see the programme

B to give Joe her opinion about last night's programme

C to see if Joe still likes the performer that she recently saw on TV

3

You must be in your seats 15 minutes before the performance begins. If you're late, you'll have to wait until the interval. Refreshments are served during the interval.

Which one of the answers below is true?

A Food and drink are included.

B You will miss the first half of the performance if you don't arrive 15 minutes early.

C The door opens 15 minutes before the start of the show.

4

Maria, I've just seen our favourite music star shopping! At first, I didn't recognise Charlie Puth. But when I did, I asked if I could take a selfie of us and he let me!

Santiago

Why has Santiago sent Maria this text message?

A to tell Maria about an unusual event that happened to him

B to check if Maria wants to see the photo he recently took of someone famous

C to let Maria know about a special event where she can meet a star

2 **You've just seen your favourite singer. Read the message and write your message.**

Guess who I just saw? Pink! She was walking into a clothes shop with her friends and I opened the door for them. I recognised her immediately because of her hair. It's amazing! She said hello and thank you to me. She's really kind! I really admire her.

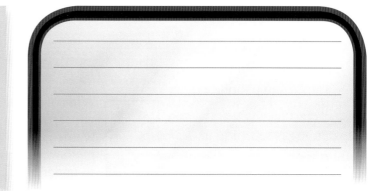

⭐ Grammar: adjectives with prepositions

1 **Complete the sentences with the correct preposition.**

> about   about   ~~for~~   in   of   of   of   on

1   David Guetta is famous ___for___ his songs with people like Black Eyed Peas and Rihana. He's also a successful DJ.

2   I'm not that interested _____ jazz, but I love disco.

3   She's tired _____ being in the studio all day. She'd rather see her fans!

4   Lucas was happy _____ being in the crowd when Shakira's car arrived.

5   He's afraid _____ photographers posting bad photos of him online!

6   Our teacher looks bored _____ saying the same thing every day. Maybe we should do our homework on time.

7   Lily's very excited _____ meeting Calvin Harris. She's so lucky!

8   Thiago is keen _____ classical music. He's been learning the violin since he was six.

2 ⭐ **Complete the text with the correct words.**

My sister Helen has always been keen **(1)** ___on___ music. She can sing beautifully and plays the flute and the piano. She used to write songs for famous people to sing, but she got tired **(2)** _____ that very quickly. She says she doesn't want to be famous **(3)** _____ her music and I know she's worried **(4)** _____ people writing things about her online. She's interested **(5)** _____ working with young people, but she doesn't want to be a teacher. So, she's decided to help people in hospitals using music – doing music therapy in a hospital. When children are ill or scared, she works with them by playing music, dancing and singing. She's very excited **(6)** _____ her new job. She knows the beneficial effect of music and has always said that music is good **(7)** _____ you!

3 **In pairs, talk about the photos.** Use the adjectives and prepositions in Activity 1.

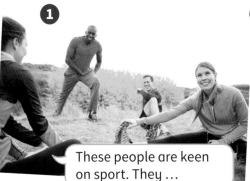

These people are keen on sport. They …

1 **Complete the descriptions with the correct adjectives.**

If you could create your perfect friend, what would they be like?

For me, a perfect friend is someone I can have fun with. He or she should be (1) cheerful and happy most of the time and he or she shouldn't be too (2) s_____ or sensible. But he or she has to be (3) r_____ too. If a friend is always late, even the funniest joke won't make me smile!

I'm lucky because my best friend, Martin, is perfect! He's (4) i_____ and gets top marks at school. He's also (5) p_____ and can explain things to me. When it's my birthday, he knows exactly what to buy me and is very (6) g_____. My parents like him because he's polite and (7) c_____. They are very fond of him. Sometimes I think they like Martin more than me!

I don't think it's possible to have a perfect friend. I have three very good friends at school and they are all perfect in different ways. Anna is good at sports, Sara is interested in the same things as me and Marta is very kind. If you aren't (8) r_____ or horrible to other people and you don't tell us what to do (we can't stand (9) b_____ people!), you can be our friend.

2 **Read the school reports and answer the questions.**

Selin is very intelligent and is always cheerful. Her exam results this year were excellent and I'm very pleased with her progress. She can, though, be a little bossy and should try to be more patient.

English	97%	Maths	83%	History	98%

Emiliano has had a good year. He finds some subjects difficult, but he works hard. He's fantastic at sports, in particular tennis. He's a reliable and popular member of the class and can be very charming.

English	70%	Maths	84%	Science	57%

1 Who is better at Maths?

2 Who got the best exam results overall this year?

3 Who would you prefer to be friends with? Why?

3 **Write a school report for your friend using the adjectives in Activity 1.**

⭐ **Grammar:** short answers with *so* and *nor*

1 Choose the correct answer.

1 I love the soundtrack to the new *Sherlock Gnomes* film. **So do I.** / **Nor do I.**

2 Richard didn't remember to bring his headphones to the gym. **So did Laura.** / **Nor did Laura.**

3 I would like to travel when I'm older. **Nor would I.** / **So would I.**

4 I'm not going to listen to the podcast. **Nor am I.** / **So am I.**

5 You swam really well at the competition at the weekend. **So did you.** / **Nor did you.**

6 Catalina hasn't eaten her piece of cake yet. **So have I.** / **Nor have I.**

2 🎧 4.03 **Listen to the conversations.** Then complete the sentences and write your answer.

1 I would rather be _____ than _____ .

2 I can't _____ a _____ to school.

3 I _____ to space. _____

4 I _____ to my party last year. _____

Speaking

B1 Preliminary for Schools ➤

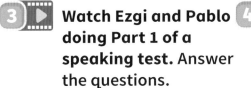

3 ▶️ **Watch Ezgi and Pablo doing Part 1 of a speaking test.** Answer the questions.

4 📝 **Now copy and plan your own answers to the questions.**

1 What question couldn't Pablo answer at first? What did the examiner do to help?

2 What topics are mentioned?

3 Who doesn't always answer the teacher's questions?

Tell us about what type of music you like.

Do you have a favourite singer or pop group?

What do you like doing in your free time?

PRONUNCIATION TIP!
Some words can sound as if they are joined to the next word like 'do you – d'you' 'going to – gonna.' It's important to be aware of this.

5 ▶️ **Watch again and complete the phrases.**

1 How _____ ?

2 Ezgi, _____ what types of music you like.

SPEAKING TIP! Listen carefully to the examiner's questions and make sure you answer what he or she is asking you.

1 **Read the sentences about the story.** Answer *yes*, *no* or *don't know*. **Explain your answers.**

1   Julie and Ash aren't interested in pop music videos.   no

      In the story it says 'What a great weekend. We spent ages lip synching to pop music videos'.

2   The competition takes place every Sunday.

3   Julie didn't have a good idea for a name for the band.

4   Julie says that each band sings its own songs.

5   Julie's dad doesn't like classical music.

6   Jasha doesn't win the competition.

2 **When Ash enters the band in the competition, Julie feels angry with her friend. Why? Discuss the three possible reasons (A–C) with a partner.**

A

Julie thought Ash wasn't listening to her.

B

Julie wanted to enter the band in the competition.

C

Julie doesn't think the competition is very interesting.

3 **How does Ash help Julie at the leisure centre?** Write your ideas below.

4 ⭐ **Write your answer in about 100 words in the space below. Read this email from your English speaking friend and the notes you have made.**

Me too!

Ask what time the concert starts

| To: | |
| From: | Ash |

Hi,

I'm so excited about Saturday! I can't believe we're doing the concert. I'm so glad you're coming. It's great that all our friends will be there.

Julie is coming to my house afterwards. Would you like to come too? We could watch a film or sing along to some videos. Which would you prefer? Or would you like to do something else?

See you on Saturday (I hope!)

Ash

Tell Ash

Suggest …

Write your email to Ash, using all your notes.

| To: | |
| From: | |

EXAM TIP! Remember to begin your email with a friendly phrase such as 'It's great to hear from you.' or 'I was so pleased to get your email.'

1 Read the texts about Beethoven and Mozart again. Answer the questions.

1 Who were their first teachers?

Their first teachers were their fathers.

2 What were their first instruments?

3 What do you think their childhood was like? Do you think it was happy and they had fun?

4 What type of problems did they have when they got older?

5 How old were they when they died?

6 How were their lives similar and how were they different?

2 Read the text. How have DJs become popular?

Beethoven and Mozart's music was played for kings and important families around Europe. Today, we can all go to concerts or listen to our favourite music at home. Music continues to change and house music is now very popular.

Not very long ago, pop singers and rock musicians were the kings and queens of music. Friends used to argue about the best band and they saved up their pocket money to buy their favourite bands' latest records. In the past, DJs simply played the music that the people asked for, but today they create the music. DJs have taken over pop culture and they are quickly becoming the new celebrities. It began in the 1990s when house music became popular. Young people, who loved to dance, were more interested in the beat or rhythm of the song than in the words. Technology has helped DJs develop this style of music. They can download the beat and the vocals and create new music easily. DJs are now as popular as the original musicians. They have thousands of fans who will travel across the country to watch them perform.

3 Find out and write about the life and music of a popular musician from your country.

Name	
Date and place of birth	
Profession	
Style of music	
Important work	

1 **For each question, choose the correct answer.**

1

NEEDED
DJs to play hip-hop music for regular customers Must be over 18 Friendly club with its own modern equipment

☐ A The club is looking for new customers.

☐ B The club is asking DJs to bring their own equipment.

☐ C The club is looking for DJs over a certain age.

2

Lorena,
Sorry if I was rude earlier. I hardly ever argue with friends. I was surprised that you didn't tell me about the dance party, that's all. Call me when you get home.
Ashley

Ashley wants Lorena

☐ A to be less rude.

☐ B to phone her later.

☐ C to tell her about the dance party.

3

Do not touch

Do not touch or pick up these instruments unless a museum officer is present

Visitors to the museum

☐ A are not allowed to hold the instruments.

☐ B can only hold the instruments when a member of staff is there.

☐ C can ask a member of staff to tell them about the instruments.

4

Kylie,
I finally met your drama teacher. He's not bossy, he was charming and patient! He told me which costume you need for the school show.
Mum   8:30

Kylie's drama teacher

☐ A spoke to Kylie's mum about the school show.

☐ B explained why he is so strict during drama lessons.

☐ C has got a costume for Kylie.

5

Drinks, snacks and hot food from the school shop must not be taken into the hall or on the stage

☐ A If you are hungry you can buy something in the hall.

☐ B You can't eat or drink on the stage but you can in the hall.

☐ C You can't eat or drink anything is this area.

My progress: ☐ /5

1 🎧 4.04 For each question, choose the correct answer.

1 Which part of the girl's body was sore recently?

A ☐   B ☐   C ☐

2 What will the children do first?

A ☐   B ☐   C ☐

3 Who did the man send the video to first?

A ☐   B ☐   C ☐

4 Which article does Bridget always read?

A ☐   B ☐   C ☐

5 Which festival did the boy enjoy the most?

A ☐   B ☐   C ☐

6 Which activity did the girl manage to do on her own at summer camp?

A ☐   B ☐   C ☐

My progress: ☐ /6

1 Choose the correct answer.

1   I'm pleased **about** / **of** / **for** winning the prize.

2   Mario is great **for** / **at** / **in** baking cakes.

3   We're ready **in** / **for** / **of** the concert.

4   This raincoat is good **for** / **at** / **about** the rain.

5   Mum was proud **with** / **for** / **of** Lucy when she heard her sing.

6   Jaime isn't interested **with** / **in** / **at** hip-hop music.

2 Match the sentences (1–6) to the answers (A–F).

1   I wouldn't want to be an opera singer.

2   I'm not very good at sport.

3   I can't play a musical instrument.

4   Helen got 10/10 in English today.

5   Tristan and Zac have got a rabbit.

6   I'll tell the teacher what happened.

A   So have I.

B   Nor can I.

C   Nor would I.

D   So will I.

E   So did I.

F   Nor am I.

3 Order the letters to make words. Complete the sentences.

sysbo   lkfo   ~~disuto~~   aoerp   iarellbe   sugereon

1   Ariana Grande is in the _____studio_____ recording a new song.

2   My sister is very _____. She always tells me what to do.

3   The _____ music festival was great. There were lots of people with guitars.

4   I don't like _____. I don't understand Italian and I can't understand the story.

5   Uncle Lucas is very _____. He buys me lots of presents.

6   James isn't _____. He's always late and he never does what he promises to do.

4 Complete the text with the correct answer.

jazz   opera   nor do we   patient   good at   so am I   ~~cheerful~~   hip-hop

This is Mrs Holt. She's my music teacher at school. I love her lessons because she's really
(1) _cheerful_ and **(2)** _____ explaining things. She's really into classical music and
(3) _____. She loves watching the performers sing as well as act. Her favourite instrument is
the trumpet, like me. She's always **(4)** _____ and positive in lessons.
We're preparing for a concert at the moment. The members of the
(5) _____ band are practising their trumpets, guitars, drums and other
instruments, the **(6)** _____ dancers are getting their performance ready,
and Sally is singing **(7)** _____ on stage. Everything is going well, but Mrs
Holt is looking a bit serious. I know she doesn't want anything to go wrong
when we're on stage and **(8)** _____!

2 Big wide world

My goal

I can answer questions about celebrations. **5**

Mission Complete!

I can read and understand information about countries around the world. **4**

I can talk about and give personal information. **3**

I can listen and complete a text with specific information. **1**

I can read and understand important information about our planet in a text. **2**

And I need ...

To do this, I will ...

So I can ...

I want to practise ...

⊙ Diary

What I already know about the world around us ...

What I have learned about the world around us ...

1 **Look at the shapes and write the names of the continents.**

1 Asia

2

3

4

5

6

7

2 🎧 **4.05** **Read and complete the facts.** **Then listen and check.**

1 The flag of _____China_____ is yellow and _____.

2 The border between the USA and _____ is the second longest in the world.

3 The capital of _____ isn't Sydney; it's Canberra.

4 _____ is made up of England, Northern Ireland, Scotland and Wales.

5 Turkey is on two continents: Asia and _____.

6 _____, which is also called Éire, celebrates St Patrick's Day.

3 **Read the information and complete the gaps.**

There are over **7,000** **(1)** l_____
in the world. There are 2,301 spoken in Asia
alone!

People of many **(2)** n_____
live in the USA. Around **50 million** people
aren't American who live there.

The Earth has a very varied
(3) c_____. Here are some
world records. The hottest temperature:
56.7˚c The coldest temperature -89.2˚c

Planet Earth has a diverse
(4) l_____ but only 43% is
habitable.
There are lots of different
(5) c_____ in the world and the
cultural diversity on our planet is amazing!

1 🎧 4.06 **You will hear a boy called Oliver talking about a trip he took with his family. Put the pictures in the correct order.**

1

2

1

3

4

5

6

2 🎧 4.07 ⭐ **Listen again. For each question, write the correct answer in the gap. Write one or two words.**

The family's trip was planned by Oliver's **(1)** _____sister_____ .

Oliver was surprised to see how popular **(2)** _____ was in Moscow.

Oliver and his family travelled from Russia to China by **(3)** _____ .

Oliver says there were about **(4)** _____ pandas in the wildlife park in Chengdu.

Oliver found it hard to get used to the **(5)** _____ in Morocco.

When he's older, Oliver would like to visit the **(6)** _____ in Morocco.

⭐ Grammar: relative clauses

1 **Complete with *who*, *which*, *whose* or *where*. Tick the sentences where *that* is also correct.**

1 I wore the blue bathing suit. You gave it to me for my birthday.

I wore the blue bathing suit _____ you gave me for my birthday. ☐

2 Chris Hemsworth is an actor. He comes from Australia.

Chris Hemsworth is an actor _____ comes from Australia. ☐

3 We stayed in the hotel. A famous chef works there.

We stayed in the hotel _____ the famous chef works. ☐

4 Thomas was speaking to the man. His daughter made the moon cakes.

Thomas was speaking to the man _____ daughter made the moon cakes. ☐

2 **Complete the non-defining relative clauses. Use *which*, *where* or *whose*.**

1 James can explain the story of the dragon dance. (His mum comes from Shanghai)

James, _____ , can explain the story of the dragon dance.

2 Grace speaks Swahili. (It's spoken by over 100 million people.)

Grace speaks Swahili, _____ .

3 Brazil is the largest country in South America. (Portuguese is spoken.)

Brazil, _____ , is the largest country in South America.

3 **Match the sentence halves (1–6) to their endings (A–F). Then complete with *who*, *which*, *whose* or *where*.**

1 The glass slipper was the object
2 Hagrid is the giant
3 Camp Nou is the stadium
4 This is Andy Murray
5 J.R.R Tolkien is the author
6 They speak Spanish

A _____ brother is also a tennis player.
B _____ is spoken by over 400 million people!
C ___which___ Cinderella lost at 12 o'clock.
D _____ wrote *The Hobbit*.
E _____ brother is called Gawp.
F _____ the Barcelona football team plays.

4 **In pairs, say defining and non-defining sentences about the following pictures.**

Paris, where the Eiffel Tower is, is …

Paris / capital city / Eiffel Tower

The White House / President of the USA

Ed Sheeran / guitar

Koke / Atlético Madrid

1 Complete the adverts with places.

Come and stay in our wonderful
(1) campsite_____ right next to
the **(2)** c_____. When
you wake up in the morning,
you can have a traditional
English breakfast in our café.
The **(3)** s_____ here is
beautiful and it's very peaceful.

If you want to travel from England to France,
you can take a ferry from Dover.
The **(4)** p_____ is just 34 km
from France and 16 million people travel from
here every year! Dover is famous for its white
(5) c_____, which you can see when
you leave the **(6)** h_____.

Lyme **(7)** B_____, which is part
of a World Heritage Site, is on the English
(8) s_____ in the south of
England. People come here to relax, eat in
the cafés and restaurants … and to look for
dinosaur fossils!

Our canoeing centre is
in the beautiful Welsh
(9) v_____.
Just push your canoe
into the river, jump
in and canoe happily
down the River Wye.
Perfect for beginners
and experts.

2 Look and complete the mind maps. In pairs, compare your ideas.

boats

port

noisy

cold   tent

campsite

rubbish

seaside

sand

3 In pairs, choose and describe one of the photos. Use the words in Activity 2 or your own ideas.

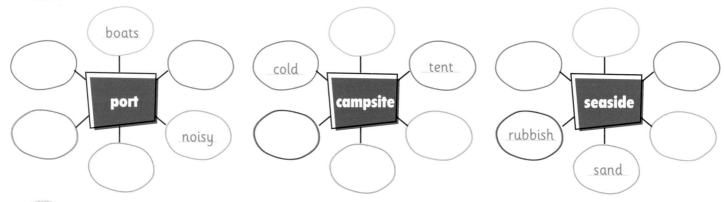

1

2

3

This is a photo of …

It looks …

It might be …

★ Grammar: *more ... than, fewer ... than, less ... than, the most, the fewest, the least*

1 **Choose the correct answer.**

1 There are *less* / *fewer* countries in South America than in Europe.
2 Sandra speaks *more* / *the most* languages than anyone I know. She's amazing!
3 She got *the fewest* / *the least* marks in the geography tests. She was very upset.
4 There's *few* / *less* noise at the campsite at night than during the day.
5 Money is *the least* / *fewest* important thing for me.
6 She is *the most* / *more* well-travelled person in my family. She's been everywhere!

2 **Write sentences with the words in the box.**

less   fewer   the least   the fewest

1 Natalia has _____ cards than Thiago.
2 Felipe has _____ cards.

3 Simba has _____ space than Rory.
4 Paws has _____ space.

Speaking

B1 Preliminary for Schools

3 **Watch Ezgi doing Part 2 of a speaking test.** Listen and number the words in order.

A at the front ☐   C on the left ☐
B in the middle ☐   D at the back ☐

5 **Imagine you're Pablo. Describe your photo. Then listen to Pablo.**

It's a / They're a type of ...

It isn't / They aren't ...

4 **In pairs, take turns to describe these things without saying the word.**

cash machine   helmet   horror film
mouse   port   rude   trainers

6 **Watch again and write four phrases to give you time to think.**

1 _____   3 _____
2 _____   4 _____

SPEAKING TIP! If you don't know the word for something, try describing it, or saying what it isn't.

1 **Answer the questions.**

1 What is the importance of coloured powder in the Holi Festival?
  The coloured paint makes everyone look the same

2 Why is the Holi Festival celebrated in so many different parts of the world?

3 Why is the festival in Thailand called The Monkey Buffet?

4 What is the importance of monkeys to the people of Thailand?

5 What do the people of Sumpango spend a lot of their free time doing?

6 What do the messages on the kites tell us about the people of Sumpango?

2 **Complete the article with the words from the box.**

~~population~~ festivities celebrates explodes Festival new

The Chinese New Year, or Spring Festival, is celebrated in Chinese communities in many different countries all over the world. One sixth of the
(1) _population_ of the world
(2) _____ the Chinese New Year. The (3) _____ starts on the first day of the
(4) _____ moon, which is always on one of the last ten days of January or on one of the first 20 days of February. People decorate the streets with red lanterns. The sky
(5) _____ with the light from thousands of fireworks, and children wear new clothes, and receive red envelopes containing gifts of money from their parents, grandparents, uncles and aunts. Every Chinese New Year is named after a different animal (the Year of the Ox, The Year of the Dragon, the Year of the Pig, etc.) The (6) _____ last for 15 days.

3 **For each question, choose the correct answer.** You will hear a radio interview about a festival.

1 The Spring Festival

   A   started last year.

   B   is new this year.

   C   is an annual event.

2 Last year everyone

   A   carried flowers.

   B   wore flower costumes.

   C   painted flowers on the floats.

3 The Spring Queen

   A   caught a bad cold.

   B   loved the flowers.

   C   had a problem with the flowers.

4 School children

   A   played with the brass band last year.

   B   are playing the music at the parade this year.

   C   are marching to the music of the brass band this year.

5 There

   A   are going to be cakes and sandwiches to eat.

   B   are going to be pies for everyone to eat.

   C   isn't going to be any food at the Festival this year.

6 The puppet shows

   A   were very popular last year.

   B   are going to be held in the Town Hall.

   C   are new this year.

1 Match the sentence halves (1–5) to their endings (A–E).

1 Ocean plants
2 If the ocean gets too warm,
3 Krill like to live
4 Sea turtles and many kinds of fish
5 Algae

A in very cold water near sea ice.
B live in coral reefs.
C make their own food like plants.
D many plants and animals will have to adapt or die.
E take in a quarter of the carbon dioxide we produce.

2 Read the text and answer the questions.

Scientists around the world have become very worried because the level of the ocean is getting higher. If the levels continue to go up, this will be a serious problem for places that are close to the sea. Why is this happening? The Earth is getting warmer because we produce a lot of carbon dioxide.

This gas stops the heat from Earth escaping back into space. As a result, the Earth's ice is melting and the level of the ocean is rising because of the extra water. We need to reduce the amount of carbon dioxide that we produce before it is too late.

Plants use carbon dioxide to make their food so we should also protect the forests and plant more trees. We should also stop using coal and oil to produce energy and start using alternative energy like solar and wind energy.

1 Why is the level of the ocean getting higher?

_____

2 Why is the Earth's ice melting?

_____

3 Why is the Earth's temperature increasing?

_____

4 Why should we plant more trees?

_____

5 What do you think will happen if the level of the oceans continues to get higher?

_____

3 Find out and complete the chart.

	Pacific Ocean	Indian Ocean	Arctic Ocean	Atlantic Ocean	Southern Ocean
How big is it?				106,500,000 square km	
How deep is it?				3,339 m	

B1: Preliminary for Schools

Work in groups of three: one examiner and two candidates, A and B.

 A and B: close your books. Speak for 2-3 minutes.

Examiner: ask questions.

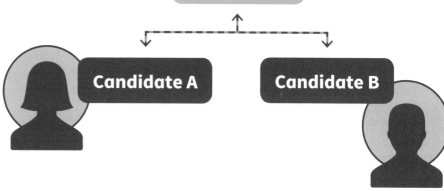

Examiner

Candidate A **Candidate B**

1 **First, ask A and B for their mark sheets and about their name, age and where they live.**

Good morning/afternoon, can I have your mark sheets, please? (pause)

A and B mime giving their mark sheets

'What's your name'? (pause)
'How old are you'? (pause)
'Thank you'.

'Where do you live'? (pause) 'Who do you live with'? (pause) 'Thank you'.

'What's your name'? (pause)
'How old are you'? (pause)
'Thank you'.

'Where do you live'? (pause) 'Who do you live with'? (pause) 'Thank you'.

2 **Then, ask about everyday routines or situations. Choose up to 4 questions each.**

Tell us about a country you've visited.

What's your favourite subject at school?

How do you prefer to travel?

What kind of music do you like listening to?

Tell us about a language you would like to learn.

How often do you travel by car?

How do you spend your time at the weekend?

Which do you like best, hot or cold weather?

Thank you.

My progress:		
I understood and answered all the questions. ☐	I understood and answered most of the questions. ☐	I didn't understand all the questions and needed some help. ☐

1 **Five sentences have been removed from the article.** For each question, choose the correct answer. There are three extra sentences which you do not need to use.

European Life

I was born in China in Beijing, the capital city. I went to the same school in the centre of the city until I was ten. **(1)** ☐ One day when I got home, my parents said they had something serious to tell me. My first thought was that they had heard I was getting terrible marks.

(2) ☐ In fact, they told me that we had a new home in Europe! I had only seen places like France and Portugal on a map and I had no idea what life would be like so far away. The more we talked about it, the more curious I became. The country was Austria and so I contacted a cousin who lived in Vienna to ask him some questions. About a week later he emailed me some photos and a description of his daily life. They made me realise how different life there was compared with China. **(3)** ☐

When the plane landed, I felt sure we'd done the wrong thing. I was already missing my friends. **(4)** ☐ . I was learning to speak German as well as English. Fortunately, my school results were improving. I didn't feel so lonely, I just felt lucky.

The truth is that I like my life more in Europe because it's easier to get to places like Italy, Greece and Spain for fantastic holidays. A lot of my Chinese friends have visited me too. Now I'm in my last year of school so I'm preparing to go to university in the UK. **(5)** ☐ I'm so glad my parents decided to move here. Even if some of the food is totally different from Beijing, I still look forward to visiting China to eat my favourite dishes at New Year. I can see my friends and visit my granny then too!

A   It was nothing about my progress in class.

B   However, a week later I had met a bunch of new people in a large, international school.

C   I was always good at maths and English.

D   I'm planning to study business when I'm there.

E   It was a small building with cheerful and patient teachers.

F   I can still remember my ninth birthday.

G   I couldn't imagine our modern apartment.

H   If he could deal with such a big change then so could I.

My progress: ☐ /5

1 Look at the pictures and complete the story with the missing phrase.

One sunny day, my parents and I were packing our car, **(1)** _____ . We were really excited because we were going to stay by the seaside **(2)** _____ . We bought a new tent too! When Mum and I were getting into the car, Dad stopped to speak to the woman **(3)** _____ . We were late so, in a hurry, we drove off. We didn't hear the key **(4)** _____ fall onto the floor. We arrived at the campsite late at night and wanted to put the tent up. My parents **(5)** _____ weren't happy when they realised they had lost the key. And the tent was in the box too! But I still had Tony my bear, so it wasn't a total disaster.

A   who lived next door

B   whose suitcases were in the box,

C   which had a box on the roof

D   where we booked a nice campsite

E   which opened the box

2 Look at the facts. Then complete the sentences.

Continent	Number of countries	Percentage of the Earth
Africa	54	20%
Asia	48	30%
Europe	46	7%
North America	4	16.5%
South America	13	12%

1   There are _____fewer_____ countries in North America than in South America.

2   There are _____ countries in Asia than in Europe.

3   The continent with the _____ space is Europe.

4   The continent with _____ countries is Africa.

5   South America has _____ space than North America.

6   North America has _____ countries in the chart.

3 In pairs, say and guess the words. Use defining or non-defining relative clauses.

nationality   climate   Australia   Antarctica
bay   campsite   port   scenery   valley

> This is a word which describes where you are from.

3 Shopping around

My goal

Mission Complete!

I can write a simple story. **5**

I can give my opinion and agree or disagree on a given topic. **4**

I can decide if sentences are true or false. **3**

I can understand a listening text. **1**

I can talk about things I did in the past related to shopping. **2**

 **Diary**

What I already know about shopping …

What I have learned about shopping …

And I need …

To do this, I will …

So I can …

I want to practise …

1 Find the words and complete the definitions.

1 how much something costs _____ price _____
2 something that is cheaper than normal

_____

3 something plastic you use to buy something now and pay later _____
4 a piece of paper to show you have paid for something _____
5 a piece of paper asking for payment

_____

6 someone who helps customers _____
7 money you get back if you gave more than necessary _____
8 notes and coins, but not cards _____

S	A	I	R	P	W	Y	E	L
H	P	B	A	R	G	A	I	N
O	H	O	T	B	T	S	K	S
P	R	I	C	E	O	C	Q	D
A	E	E	E	S	D	R	Y	O
S	C	H	A	N	G	E	W	B
S	E	B	N	E	W	D	B	I
I	I	S	S	M	R	I	A	L
S	P	F	R	I	S	T	H	L
T	T	G	E	C	H	C	W	K
A	A	Z	Y	C	P	A	E	P
N	J	C	A	S	H	R	Y	U
T	O	I	O	V	R	D	U	X

2 Look at the exchange rate and the photos. Complete the receipts.

EXCHANGE RATE
For £1, you can buy …

country	currency	rate
Europe	EUR	1.15
US	USD	1.5
Australia	AUD	1.7

£1.25

£10

£20

£5

THANK YOU FOR YOUR CUSTOM

2 x magnets
1 x hoodie (L)
1 £ _____
paid in US dollars = 2 $ _____
cash $40
change 3 $ _____

PLEASE CALL AGAIN!

1 x teddy
1 x Big Ben statue
4 £ _____
paid in EUR = 5 € _____
cash 20€
change 6 € _____

3 You have 20 Australian dollars. In pairs, talk about what you'd like to buy.

| Australia | AUD | 1.7 |

I'd like to buy …

Find someone who …

paid a very high price for something. _____

got something for a bargain. _____

paid for something by card. _____

bought something yesterday. _____

bought something they didn't need. _____

bought something they regret. _____

tried to change something but didn't have the receipt. _____

bought something using dollars. _____

2 ⭐ **Read the text below and choose the correct word for each space.**

A bank that deals with cheese

To most people, Parmesan cheese is just a delicious cheese to have with pasta. However, some Italians **(1)** _____ it to be as valuable as gold.

If that sounds **(2)** _____ , then think about how much cheese Italy actually produces. It's the biggest cheese producer in the world, while Parmesan is one of its most popular cheeses. Since Parmesan takes two years before it's ready to eat, cheesemakers often experience financial **(3)** _____ before it's ready to sell and can't afford to buy ingredients to make more cheese.

Since 1953, the Credito Emiliano bank has **(4)** _____ cheesemakers to bring in their Parmesan cheese wheels to get loans. The bank keeps the cheese in specially built rooms until a cheesemaker has **(5)** _____ back the loan.

This unusual Italian bank has been a great **(6)** _____ in helping cheesemakers grow their business while the bank looks after their Parmesan cheese that's worth its weight in gold.

1	A respect	B consider	C feel	D recognise
2	A unforgettable	B hopeless	C challenging	D impossible
3	A issues	B effects	C situations	D disadvantages
4	A accepted	B applied	C allowed	D admitted
5	A put	B paid	C taken	D sent
6	A effort	B gain	C progress	D success

⭐ **Grammar: verbs + gerund and verbs + infinitive**

1 **Choose the correct answer.**

1 Lucas wants (to buy) / *buying* something for his sister's birthday.

2 Alba didn't promise *to sell* / *selling* me her bike.

3 Fiona and I fancy *to watch* / *watching* something at the cinema tonight.

4 Asil doesn't mind *to do* / *doing* the washing-up.

5 We plan *to travel* / *travelling* around Asia next year.

6 My mum gave up *to learn* / *learning* to drive when she went round the roundabout the wrong way!

2 **Complete the text with the correct form of the verbs.**

| be be ~~watch~~ get buy win hit watch |

I love **(1)** _watching_ tennis and one day I would like **(2)** _____ as good as Nadal! When I was in my first year at this school, I asked **(3)** _____ on the school team. Last year I lost one of my matches, but won ten. This year I hope **(4)** _____ them all! I love being outdoors and I practise **(5)** _____ the ball over the net and before the line hundreds of times a day, but I hate **(6)** _____ up early for my tennis lessons. I love **(7)** _____ people like Federer and Kyrgios play, but tickets to tennis matches are very expensive. My dad always agrees **(8)** _____ tickets for us as we're both big tennis fans!

3 📝 **Write sentences using one word from each column.**

imagine	write	chocolate cake for breakfast
finish	wear	trumpet
fancy	get	letter to Santa
learn	be	mouse costume
need	play	100%
fail	eat	unicorn

4 **In pairs, compare your sentences from Activity 3. Whose are the most interesting?**

My first sentence is 'Can you imagine being a unicorn?'

I said 'I fancy getting a unicorn for my birthday.' I prefer your sentence.

1 **Read and complete with the words in the box.**

spend reduced ~~second hand~~ for sale exchange cost return	
sold damaged reasonable luxury sale	

When I was younger, my family didn't have much money, but we were very happy. This is me at my first dance class. My shoes were **(1)** _second hand_ and very dirty. They used to belong to my sister, but they were a bit **(2)** _____ at the front.

We usually shopped in charity shops when I was little, but occasionally we bought clothes in the **(3)** _____ . I remember my mum buying me this dress for my birthday. I think it was **(4)** _____ .

The problem with buying things in the sale is that sometimes you can't **(5)** _____ them for something else, or **(6)** _____ them

to get your money back. My grandparents are very generous with their grandchildren. They bought these jeans for my brother, but he didn't try them on first. He looks very silly!

When I was 13, my mum got a new job and we had more money. Suddenly we were able to **(7)** _____ more money on things we liked. We found a beautiful house that was **(8)** _____ , so we **(9)** _____ our old one. We went on holidays abroad every year and stayed in **(10)** _____ hotels. I'm not sure how much the holidays **(11)** _____ , but we had lots of fun. We stayed in this hotel in India. It's beautiful, isn't it?

My favourite possession is a bracelet I bought last year. It looks really expensive, but it was quite **(12)** _____ .

2 🎧 4.09 **Listen to the conversations. Read and tick the correct sentence.**

1 A   The shop assistant is going to exchange the laptop. ☐

   B   The boy doesn't have a receipt for the laptop. ☐

2 A   Hannah thinks the price is reasonable. ☐

   B   Cara doesn't think the boots cost too much. ☐

3 A   The guitar is cheap because it was damaged. ☐

   B   The guitar is cheap because it isn't new. ☐

4 A   The girl can exchange the little dog if he isn't friendly. ☐

   B   The girl can't buy the dog she wants. ☐

⭐ Grammar: gerunds as subjects and objects

1 **Complete the sentences with the correct form of the verb in the box**

swim   look   ~~play~~   shop   have   eat

1   ___Playing___ computer games every day is boring.

2   Lucia isn't happy about _____ a test on her birthday.

3   _____ on Saturday is my sister's favourite hobby. She always buys a lot!

4   _____ fruit for breakfast is a good idea.

5   _____ for bargains in shops is a way of saving money.

6   I'm not interested in _____. I hate getting wet.

2 **In pairs, order the words to make sentences.**

1   about   The best   cycling   is that   thing   quickly.   you can get home

2   thing about   is that   washing-up   too busy to help.   The worst   my sister is always

3   Japan   on   when I'm older.   visiting   I'm keen

4   doing   a good idea!   Not   for Mr Thomas   your homework   is not

5   a film   a good suggestion.   tonight   Watching   is

Speaking

B1 Preliminary for Schools ➤

3 ▶ **Watch Ezgi and Pablo doing Part 3 of a speaking test. Complete the table.**

Agreeing	Disagreeing	Giving your own opinion
agree		

4 **Look at the photos again and discuss the five ideas. Which one would you choose?**

5 ▶ **Watch again and <u>underline</u> which word is stressed in each phrase in Activity 3.**

PRONUNCIATION TIP! The tone of your voice is important, so be aware how you sound when discussing things.

SPEAKING TIP! Use different phrases to express your opinion. Always remember to be polite.

1 **What is the main idea of the story?** <u>Underline</u> the correct option.

A   It is about people who follow banknotes.

B   It is about the journey of a banknote.

C   It is about valuing a gift you get.

2 **What journey did the banknote take?** Look and draw lines.

3 **Read the sentences.** Answer *yes* or *no*.

1   Churchill was a famous politician.   yes

2   Churchill was born on 30th November, 1874.   _____

3   Banknotes with unusual serial numbers are sometimes valuable.   _____

4   Tom's dad liked to collect banknotes when he was a boy.   _____

5   Tom bought the five-pound note online.   _____

6   Tom now collects unusual banknotes.   _____

4 **Match the words from the text (1–6) to their meanings (A–F).**

1   valuable   A   to connect to a computer system

2   log in   B   to pause

3   look at   C   worth a lot of money

4   calmly   D   to become visible

5   appeared   E   think about something carefully

6   took a deep breath   F   quiet, peaceful

5 **Read the advert and the example.** Then answer the questions.

ARTICLES WANTED FOR SCHOOL MAGAZINE!

My pocket money

How much pocket money do you get?
What do you like to spend your money on?
Do you buy second hand things?
Do you always look for a bargain?
Do you save any money?

We will print the most interesting and funny answers in the school magazine. Mail stories to asimpson@grimmcollege.org

---

How I spend my pocket money!

My mum and dad give me five pounds pocket money every week if I do all my homework and keep my room tidy. I get extra if I do the washing-up.

I am quite responsible, so the first thing I do is divide it in half. I take one half to school and spend it in the school shop. Sometimes I buy a sandwich or a drink. The other half I save for special things. For example, if I want a new video game, music, clothes or to go to the cinema with my friends. When I get money on my birthday or at Christmas I save it, too.

I love spending my pocket money but I love saving part of it too.

---

1 What does the first paragraph talk about? _____

2 What does the second paragraph talk about? _____

3 What does the last sentence talk about? _____

6 **Use the following tips and write your article in about 100 words.**

- Write a title
- Say how much pocket money you get and why

- Say what you spend it on
- Say how you feel about what you do with your pocket money

1 Match the sentence halves (1–5) to their endings (A–E).

1 The goldsmith gave the owner
2 In the 1950s credit cards
3 Shells were used
4 Bartering meant that
5 Gold was heavy

A you could exchange items.
B in China to pay for things.
C a receipt for the gold.
D and difficult to carry.
E were invented.

2 What would you exchange for these things? Choose from the photos.

1 a pair of jeans
2 a bar of your favourite chocolate
3 a comic or magazine
4 a basketball or football
5 a banana

3 Write about your country's money.

1 What is it called? _____
2 Which coins does it use? _____
3 Which banknotes does it use? _____
4 What is the smallest coin and what is the largest banknote? _____
5 Where is the money made? _____

4 Design a banknote for your class.

Remember:
Banknotes are made on special paper. They have complicated patterns to stop copying.

They have a secret line called a water mark.
Write the value on the note.

Work in groups of three: one examiner and two candidates, A and B.

A and B: listen to the examiner and then speak for 2-3 minutes.

Examiner: read and then listen to A and B speak. Use a timer.

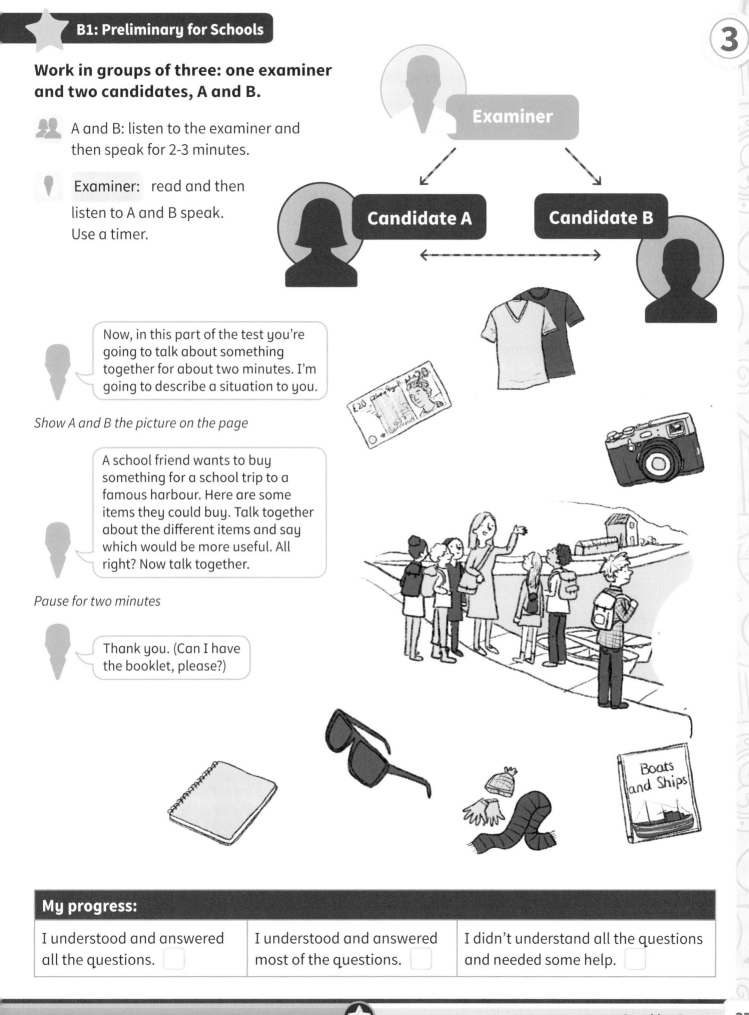

Examiner

Candidate A   Candidate B

Now, in this part of the test you're going to talk about something together for about two minutes. I'm going to describe a situation to you.

Show A and B the picture on the page

A school friend wants to buy something for a school trip to a famous harbour. Here are some items they could buy. Talk together about the different items and say which would be more useful. All right? Now talk together.

Pause for two minutes

Thank you. (Can I have the booklet, please?)

Boats and Ships

My progress:

| I understood and answered all the questions. ☐ | I understood and answered most of the questions. ☐ | I didn't understand all the questions and needed some help. ☐ |

1 **For each question, write the correct answer.** Write <u>one</u> word for each gap.

My favourite market

I love to look for bargains at the second-hand market in my town. I've saved loads of money by doing most of my shopping there. That means I can spend the rest of my pocket money on other things, such **(1)**… going out with my friends! The market is always busy because it's in the centre **(2)**… town in a really nice area along the canal. Every day there are **(3)**… least fifty different stalls that sell various used goods.

When I want to buy some second-hand designer clothes I'll see what's at the market. I know the best time to get the best deals on clothes **(4)**… before nine o'clock. That's because the **(5)**… reasonable items are always sold by midday! After I finish shopping, I'll often go to a popular café beside the market where I can get a sandwich and coffee for less **(6)**… five euros.

1 ☐☐☐☐☐

2 ☐☐☐☐☐

3 ☐☐☐☐☐

4 ☐☐☐☐☐

5 ☐☐☐☐☐☐

6 ☐☐☐☐☐

My progress: ☐ /6

1 Complete the sentences with the correct form of the verb.

~~buy~~ not put speak visit play return

1 Iker would like ___to buy___ a luxury house with a football pitch.
2 Yuck! My sister promised _____ jelly in my shoes, but look!
3 My puppy loves _____ with my socks.
4 Martina doesn't mind _____ her elderly neighbour every Sunday. He bakes nice cakes!
5 I agreed _____ Noa's library books.
6 Kim and I hoped _____ to our PE teacher after school, but she was too busy.

2 Complete the sentences with the correct form of the verbs in brackets.

1 ___Watching___ films and _____ hot chocolate is my favourite activity when it's cold and raining. (watch / drink)
2 _____ is fun if you have a good bike and don't mind going up hills! (cycle)
3 I'm not happy about _____ the washing-up again. It's your turn! (do)
4 Not _____ your change before leaving a shop is a bad idea. (check)
5 _____ a tie to my party isn't necessary. (wear)
6 I'm keen on _____ to the park with my friends to hang out at the weekends. (go)

3 Complete the sentences.

1 I need a size 38. I'll ask the ___shop___ assistant.
2 Here's your change and your r_____ .
3 My new smartphone wasn't too expensive. It was actually quite r_____ .
4 Last week this skirt cost £22, but yesterday it was r_____ to £11 in the sale.
5 How many e_____ does a train ticket from Huelva to Jaen cost?
6 Oh no! These trainers are d_____ , but they're the only ones in the shop. I don't want to buy them.

4 Find somebody in your class who …

1 has exchanged something for something else.
2 knows whose head is on a British pound coin.
3 has a receipt in their bag.
4 prefers to read books than watch films.
5 likes horse riding.
6 is keen on food shopping.

5 Imagine you bought one of these items today. You regret buying it. Say:

how much it cost
why you bought it
why you regret(ed) buying it
what you did / you're going to do now

The T-shirt cost …

Review • • • Units 1–3

1 Match the sentence halves (1–6) to their endings (A–F).

1 Yoda is famous
2 Harry would love
3 I was speaking to someone
4 There are fewer
5 Lucia promised
6 The best thing about Asia

A who comes from Australia.
B for speaking in a strange way.
C is the amazing variety of culture.
D to buy me a toy penguin.
E to be a Jedi. So would I.
F than 25,000 polar bears in the wild.

2 Complete the sentences.

1 ___Learning___ to speak other languages is important if you want to travel.

2 There are more people in the capital city _____ in my village.

3 'I've been to North America twice.' 'So _____ I! The US and Canada.'

4 Jinpin, _____ sells second-hand clothes in our town, is always very cheerful.

5 I'm not keen _____ walking by the canal. It smells horrible!

6 I hate _____ coffee at night.

3 Find the mistake in each sentence. Rewrite the sentences correctly.

1 Africa is an amazing continent which you can see wild animals and beautiful scenery.

   Africa is an amazing continent where you can see wild animals and beautiful scenery.

2 Do you plan do your homework tonight?

   _____

3 Lucy's the shop assistant which helped me choose some shoes.

   _____

4 A DJ is a person plays music.

   _____

5 I enjoy runing when it's cold.

   _____

6 We stop listening to music at 11 pm last night.

   _____

4 Order the letters. Label the pictures.

fiecrtictsae
chsa
dagedma
cotsa

1 **Look at the task.** Think about a story.

- Your English teacher has asked you to write a story.
- Your story must begin with this sentence:

My parents both looked really excited when they gave me the envelope at breakfast.

2 **Read Kamile's story.**

My parents both looked really excited when they gave me the envelope at breakfast. Inside was a birthday card with a picture of a piece of old rock. I was surprised because it was an unusual choice of card for me. Then some American dollars fell out with a note saying 'This is for you to spend when we get there.' As I live in England, US dollars aren't very useful. My mum laughed at how confused I looked and gave me some new hiking boots. 'Can you guess where we're going?' she asked. Then it all became clear. 'The Grand Canyon!' I cried. It was the best birthday surprise ever.

3 **Which two adjectives does Kamile use to show emotions?**

EXAM TIP! It's a good idea to think about how the main characters show how they feel.

4 **Complete the sentences with the words in the box.**

amazed   cheerful   surprised   terrified

1   I was so _____ of swimming with sharks that I cried every night for a week before we left.

2   Matthew's usually a very _____ person and he is always smiling.

3   Jess didn't expect to see Martin there and was so _____ she couldn't speak.

4   My mum was so _____ when she heard they were getting married that she bought them a present.

5 **Now answer the question in Activity 1.** Use adjectives to say how your characters were feeling.

Write your story in about 100 words.

_____

_____

_____

_____

_____

4 Getting about

Mission Complete!

My goal

I can read and understand a text about a famous person. **5**

I can have a conversation about travelling and holidays. **4**

I can answer questions on a story about time travel. **3**

I can do a word puzzle. **2**

I can talk about items using different tenses. **1**

And I need ...

To do this, I will ...

So I can ...

I want to practise ...

⊛ Diary

What I already know about travelling and transport ...

What I have learned about travelling and transport ...

1 Look and complete the sentences.

1 Do you think Toby's going to t a k e o f f ?

2 Amelia's got her b _ _ _ r d _ _ _ g p _ _ _ s ready.

3 Salvador has found a nice watch in the d _ t _ _ f r _ _ _ _ shop at the airport.

2 DORTMUND	ON TIME
26 DUBLIN	ON TIME
12 WARSAW	ON TIME
76 MUNICH	DELAYED
8 MUNICH	DELAYED
2 COPENHAGEN	ON TIME
02 COPENHAGEN	ON TIME

4 The f _ _ _ _ g h _ to Munich is going to be late.

5 The plane is going to l _ _ _ d near the beach.

6 The p _ _ l _ _ t s are flying the plane.

2 Find the words and answer the questions.

e̶c̶h̶k̶c̶n̶i̶   r t d p a u e r s e   t a e g

a c h e x e n g e t r a   i v a a r r s l   e n o u a n t n c e n m

1 What do you do before you go through security? _____check in_____

2 Which part of the airport does a flight leave from? _____

3 What do you have to walk through to get to your aeroplane? _____

4 What tells you how many dollars you can buy for 100 euros? _____

5 Where in an airport can you meet friends coming from another country? _____

6 What should you listen for in airports? _____

3 Complete the messages with words from Activities 1 or 2.

1 I spoke to the _____ at the door of the plane. She's called Francesca and her favourite plane to fly is the Boeing 747.

2 The _____ at the airport isn't very good. Remember to change your money before you leave home.

1 🎧 **4.10** **Listen to the interview. Circle the words that you don't hear.**

flight   jetlag   first-aid   take off   arrivals   pilot
passenger   safety   boarding pass   departures

2 🎧 **4.11** **Listen to the interview again and choose the correct answers.**

1   When Karl started to work as a flight attendant

A   he saw it as a good way to use his language skills.

B   he thought he would do it for a limited period.

C   he was keen to go to many different places.

2   What surprised some people about Karl's flight attendant training?

A   how short it was

B   where it took place

C   what subjects it covered

3   At the start of a flight, Karl gets annoyed with passengers who

A   have too much luggage.

B   want to change seats.

C   ask lots of questions.

4   What does Karl think he is particularly good at?

A   communicating with people

B   managing his time

C   solving problems

5   Karl says people are wrong if they think that flight attendants

A   have fun when they're working.

B   see a lot of the world.

C   earn good money.

6   Karl thinks he should spend more of his free time

A   developing certain skills.

B   meeting people.

C   keeping fit.

3 **In pairs, say why/why not you would/wouldn't like to be a flight attendant.**

I would love to be a flight attendant because I would be able to travel everywhere!

Grammar: review of passive forms

1 Complete the sentences with the correct form of the verb in brackets.

1 'We are sorry to announce that all flights to Australia ___have been cancelled___ today.' (cancel)
2 The final announcement _____ yet. Quick – let's run! (not make)
3 A boarding pass _____ to every passenger at check in. Don't lose it! (give)
4 Headphones _____ on the plane. Remember to bring some if you want to watch a film. (not provide)
5 We _____ at security because I had a plastic snake in my bag. (stop)
6 This photo of my uncle flying a plane _____ by my grandfather. (take)

2 Complete the second sentences so that they mean the same as the first. Use the passive.

1 We make this ice cream with eggs, sugar, cream and broccoli.
   This ice cream ___is made___ with eggs, sugar, cream and broccoli.

2 Sarah has opened Sally's present!
   Sally's present _____ Sarah!

3 I'm sorry, but we haven't found your bag or coat.
   I'm sorry, but your bag and coat _____.

4 I lost my boarding pass somewhere between check in and the gate.
   My boarding pass _____ somewhere between check in and the gate.

5 We don't wear swimsuits to school.
   Swimsuits _____ to school.

6 I didn't tell Diego and Mateo about my birthday party.
   Diego and Mateo _____ about my birthday party.

3 In pairs, choose one of the objects. Make three passive sentences.

present (it is used …)   present perfect (it has been used …)   past simple (it was used …)

money box

> This is a money box. It is used to contain coins. It was made in a factory. It has been broken into small pieces.

1 boat

2 toy

3 washing machine

4 hockey stick

5 boots

1 **Look and complete the crossword.** Write a form of transport using the yellow letters.

			1					
2								
		3						
4								

The form of transport is ⁵_____.

2 **Read and complete the signs.**

Open your (1) _passport_ at the page with the photo. Thank you!

Joe's (2) _____ Hostel: ten-bed rooms available here. Lots of space for rucksacks. Breakfast included!

Remember to be at the bus stop ten minutes early. Your (3) _____ Helena will be waiting to welcome you!

Only two pieces of (4) _____ per person on the bus.

Don't eat fast food in the (5) _____. There are specific eating areas in other parts of the station.

isaac travel reading

Never travel without information on the country you're visiting. To buy (6) _____ to all countries in Asia, please go to www.isaacstravelreading.com

Attention all drivers or lorries and other tall vehicles! Please DON'T use the (7) _____.

3 **Find five differences.** Write sentences.

_____

_____

_____

Grammar: phrasal verbs and the object

1 **Write the words in the correct gap.** Cross out the gap you don't need.

> us   baking   his little sister   ~~the dog~~   your seatbelt   talking

1 It was raining, so I kept _____the dog_____ in the house ✗ .
2 I was late because my neighbour kept _____ on _____ .
3 Our son, Richard, checked _____ in _____ before we went to the airport.
4 Put _____ on _____ , We're going to take off.
5 At the weekend, James looks _____ after _____ .
6 Next year, I'm going to take _____ up _____ .

2 **Order the words to make sentences.** There are two possible answers but write one.

1 give / of / Please / end / back / the day. / gloves / my / by / the

2 a / remember / very / can't / where! / important thing / I / put / but / away / I

3 throw away / my / Don't / passport!

4 TV / you / off / bed. / the / before / Turn / go to

Speaking

B1 Preliminary for Schools →

3 **Watch Pablo and Ezgi doing Part 4 of a speaking test.** Complete the sentences.

1 _____ , I like travelling by plane.
2 There are lots of things to see in my country, _____ , interesting towns …
3 … beautiful landscapes, seaside, _____ .
4 _____ , er, Italy I think.

4 **Now plan your answers to the questions.**

How do you like to travel when you go on holiday?

Where would you like to go on holiday next?

What do you like to take with you when you travel?

5 **Watch again and (circle) the stressed words.**

1 Well, I like travelling by plane.
2 I think I would rather go to a different country.
3 I like to travel by boat or train. I'm scared of flying.

PRONUNCIATION TIP!
When expressing your preferences, stress the noun.

1 **How do you think the characters in the story feel?** Use sentences from the story to explain your answers.

1 How do the Farmars feel when they arrive at the airport?

2 How does Billy feel when he sees the Samurai and the Ninja?

3 How does the pilot feel when he tells the Farmars he's run out of time-travelling petrol?

4 How does Carla feel when the pilot explains that they're stuck in Feudal Japan?

2 **What do you think happens in the next chapter of the novel?** In pairs, discuss your ideas.

1 Billy finds out that the people in the town can actually see him.

2 Carla finds a way to make time-travelling petrol and the family fly on to the Triassic to see the dinosaurs.

3 The pilot finds a way to make time-travelling petrol, but flies away on his own, leaving the Farmars in Feudal Japan.

4 More time-travellers arrive in the town. They have extra time-travelling petrol on their plane.

FACT!

In 1895, the English writer HG Wells published the science-fiction novel *The Time Machine*. Wells was not the first to write about time travel, but he made going backwards and forwards through time in a special vehicle a popular idea in stories. 'Time machine' is the phrase Wells used to describe the vehicle in his story. Writers, scientists and film-makers still use it today.

3 **Read and answer the questions.**

1 Would you rather travel into the future or into the past?

2 If you could go back in time, which period of history would you go to and why?

Five sentences have been removed from the article. For each question, choose the correct answer. There are three extra sentences which you do not need to use.

Have you heard of CHRONOS AIRWAYS? I'm sure you have. After all, it's the only airline in the world that gives you the chance to travel backwards and forwards in time! **(1)** ☐ We went into the future to the Year 2101. I still can't believe we did it.

When my friend Elaine Farmar first told me about CHRONOS, I thought she was joking. I've read *The Time Machine* and seen the *Back to the Future* films, but I've never thought that any of it was possible. Time travel is science fiction, isn't it? However, when Elaine showed me the family's round-time tickets and told me about their plans to go to Peru to the Age of the Incas I realised she was telling me the truth. **(2)** ☐ I just couldn't get it out of my mind, so I booked tickets to travel into the future.

Travelling with CHRONOS is just like travelling with any other airline. You go to an airport, get on a plane, sit in your seat, fasten your seatbelts and wait to take off. Everything is normal. **(3)** ☐ Somehow you have travelled in time. When we landed, in 2101, we realised straight away that we were entering a new world. **(4)** ☐ However, when they spoke they sounded just like you or me.

One of the most interesting things were the talking screens. They were in the walls, the trees and the chairs. **(5)** ☐ You'll have to travel to the future and find out for yourself. However, let me tell you this – it's going to be very interesting!

A I don't want to say too much about the screens and what they do.

B But when you land everything is different.

C Last spring my family and I went on a trip with them.

D We didn't believe them.

E I think everyone wanted the same thing.

F From that moment on, it was the only thing I could think of.

G There weren't people at the airport, only robots.

H I decided not to say anything to them.

EXAM TIP! Read the sentences before and after each gap very carefully. They will help you decide the right sentence to fill the gap.

1 **Correct the sentences about Amy Johnson.**

1   Amy Johnson was an American pilot.

2   She left London to fly to Australia on 1st July 1930.

3   Amy had to fly during the night to try to break the record.

4   She lost a lot of days because of engine problems.

5   She took fifteen days to fly from London to Australia.

2 **Look at Amy's route on the map.** Circle the countries she flew over.

London – Vienna – Constantinople (Istanbul) – Bagdad – Karachi – Calcutta –Bangkok – Singapore – Port Darwin

3 **In pairs, match the countries to the cities.**

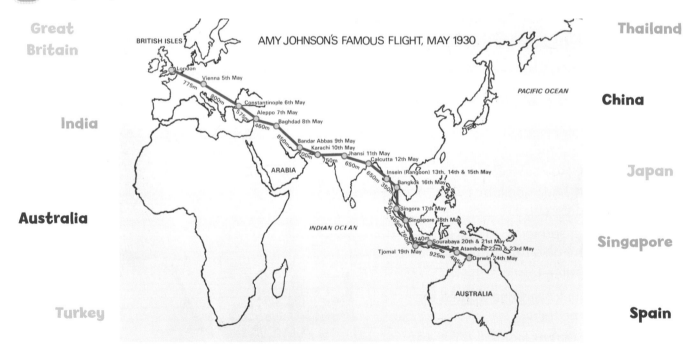

4 **Write different ways you can travel in the air.**

1 For each question, choose the correct answer.

The young people below all want to go abroad to a summer camp in Canada. Decide which summer camp would be the most suitable for the following people. For questions 1–5, mark the correct letter (A–H).

1 Yolanda wants a summer camp that offers challenging cycling trips with an expert who'll give her cycling tips. She also has plenty of experience with horses and wants to be able to go horse riding.

2 Lucas is looking at a summer camp that's at least a month long. He wants to play team sports and see professional athletes competing.

3 Maya wants a camp that offers daily yoga sessions. She's is an experienced diver who wants an instructor's advice to help her progress from intermediate to advanced dives.

4 Haruto enjoys getting involved in team activities while spending time in nature. He'd like to learn how to camp in challenging outdoor conditions and learn some historical facts about the local culture.

5 Katrin's an excellent surfer and wants a camp where she can surf and try out other extreme sports. She'd also like to take part in a project that's helping the environment.

Canadian Summer Camps

A Camp-Connect teaches teenagers how to stay safe, warm and well-fed while camping and hiking through an ancient forest in Western Canada. It's essential you like working in a group to achieve these extremely important skills. Camp leaders will also discuss the traditions of native Indians who come from this area.

B Camp Horizon is perfect for teens who love doing outdoor activities. You'll have access to a large network of easy to advance paths for hiking and horse and bike riding. Go on daily rides with national champion, Lorraine Ross, who'll give personal advice on how to improve your bike riding technique.

C Tide's Up is a one-month surfing camp for the less experienced surfer. You'll start on gentle waves until you progress to the next level. You'll also develop team map reading skills on some challenging forest hikes.

D Camp Canuck offers a wide range of individual and team sports. The facilities are suitable for learning basic horse-riding skills and for going on easy historical trail rides. Volleyball and hiking expeditions are just a few of the many activities on offer.

E Kool Kamp is for teenagers who want to improve their basketball and soccer skills. You'll follow a strict training schedule with coaches advising you, so you keep improving. It's not all hard work though! You'll go to several professional matches over this six-week camp.

F Camp Tofino is a fun-filled month-long camp. Wake up to catch waves at one of Canada's best surfing locations followed by daily windsurfing and rock-climbing lessons with local experts. An interest in protecting sea life is essential because you'll be looking after rescued leatherback turtles that are in danger.

G Coquihalla Camp is perfect for cyclists, at any level, who want qualified coaches to help them improve at cycling. Expect healthy eating and daily yoga sessions as part of the training programme at this 6-week camp.

H The Wildteen Camp is a 3-week camp for teens who are confident at either surfing, diving or sailing. All highly qualified water sport coaches will give you the support you need in order to improve to the next level in your chosen sport. Wake up to morning yoga before riding some waves.

My progress: /5

Work in groups of three: one examiner and two candidates, A and B.

 A and B: close your books and listen to the examiner.

 Examiner: read and use a timer.

Examiner

Candidate A   **Candidate B**

Now I'd like each of you to talk on your own about something. I'm going to give each of you a photograph and I'd like you to talk about it.

Listen to B for 1 minute

Thank you. (Can I have the booklet, please?)

A, here is your photograph. It shows someone getting ready for a trip. B you just listen.

Show candidate A picture 1

A, please tell us what you can see in your photograph.

Listen to A for 1 minute

Thank you. (Can I have the booklet, please?)

B, here is your photograph. It shows someone helping someone. A you just listen.

Show candidate B picture 2

B, please tell us what you can see in your photograph.

My progress:		
I understood and answered all the questions. ☐	I understood and answered most of the questions. ☐	I didn't understand all the questions and needed some help. ☐

④

1 **Write sentences using the words and the correct form of the verb.**

1 Delicious spicy curry / make / in this restaurant
Delicious spicy curry is made in this restaurant.

2 All flights / to Canada / cancel / today

3 Tennis / not play / with a basketball

4 The Eiffel Tower / complete / 1889

5 The backpacker's passport / not find / yet

6 We / not invite / to Michael's birthday

2 **Complete the sentences with the correct words in the box.**

give   plane   it   them   find   back   hamster   up   for   takes   down   out

1 It's my passport –   give   it   back   ! Please don't look at the photo!
2 I can't find my headphones anywhere. Can you help me to look _____ , please?
3 Sit down, please. The _____ off in five minutes.
4 Put my _____ , please. She doesn't like being held. Oh dear. Did she bite you?
5 Look at the kitchen! Why is there flour on the floor? Clean _____ NOW!
6 I'm sorry I don't know when the plane to Timbuktu leaves. I'll _____ now.

3 **Read and write the word.**

1 This is a person who has studied for a long time and is now in charge of a plane.   Pilot
2 If you have a bad accident, this will take you to the hospital very quickly. _____
3 This is the part of the building where planes take off from. _____
4 This person carries all of his or her things in a large bag and travels to different places. _____
5 This tells you how many pounds you can buy for your euros. _____
6 This person knows a lot about a place and explains things to visitors. _____

4 **In pairs, answer the questions.**

What do you put in your hand luggage before you go on holiday?   I always put my …

Think of a film or book with an airport in it. What happens?   I like the film *Home Alone*. The family …

Would you like to be a pilot? Why? / Why not?   I wouldn't want to be a pilot because …

5 Study smarter

My goal

Mission Complete!

I can write an article about projects for a school website. **5**

I can ask for clarification in a conversation. **4**

I can read and understand a text about an environmental project. **3**

I can read and understand adverts or notes. **1**

I can read a text and identify the missing sentences. **2**

What I already know about studying techniques …

_____

_____

What I have learned about studying techniques …

_____

_____

_____

And I need …

_____

_____

_____

To do this, I will …

_____

_____

_____

So I can …

_____

_____

_____

I want to practise …

_____

_____

_____

1 Read and complete the crossword.

Down

1 A piece of paper you can get when you pass an exam.

Across

2 If you're a beginner, you start at … 1.

3 This is a detailed piece of work with pictures and photos. It's usually done in groups.

4 These are at the top of a test paper. They tell you what to do.

5 This is how many questions you get right in a test.

6 This is a written piece of work about a specific topic.

```
        1 c
    2   e
        r
3       t
        i
        f
    4   i
        c
    5   a
        t
    6   e
```

2 Read and complete the texts.

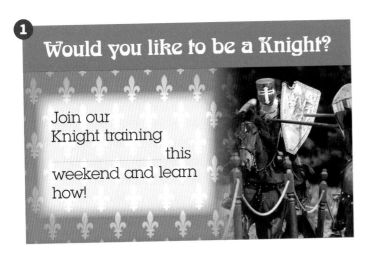

1

Would you like to be a Knight?

Join our Knight training _____ this weekend and learn how!

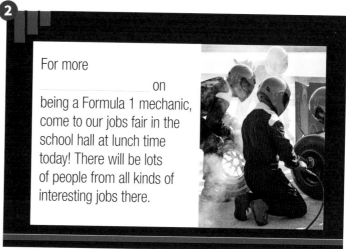

2

For more _____ on being a Formula 1 mechanic, come to our jobs fair in the school hall at lunch time today! There will be lots of people from all kinds of interesting jobs there.

3

Choose your after-school activities for the summer _____. There are a lot of things to enjoy before the summer holidays. There's a choice of cricket, athletics and water skiing on the lake. Not interested in sport? Take a look at the website for other indoor options including filmmaking and a book club.

4

Remember your history

_____

tomorrow. I expect top marks, no excuses!

Love, Mum

1 ⭐ **Five sentences have been removed from the article.** For each gap, choose the correct sentence. There are three extra sentences which you do not need to use.

The Memory Competition

It was a cold and grey morning when our teacher Mr Holmes announced that our school would compete in the Junior Memory Championship. **(1)** _____ 'Do you know, Clara I've got a great memory', said my friend Emily. 'I know all the times tables up to 14 times 14.'

'That's nothing', said Kyle. 'I always get 10 out of 10 in my spelling tests, don't I, Clara?'.

'I know you both have a good memory', I said. 'Quiet now', said Mrs Frank, our class teacher. 'I'll set you some challenges and the two best students can go to the competition.'

We spent the rest of the term doing memory tests. I learned the names of trees, the dates of kings and queens and lots and lots of phone numbers. **(2)** _____
'I imagine numbers as pictures. So for me, the number five is a hand, because we have four fingers and a thumb on a hand,' explained Kyle.

'That sounds very complicated,' I said. 'I like to sing the numbers when I walk to school.'

'I suppose we all learn in different ways. I use pictures, you use songs.'

(3) _____ 'Clara and Mario have got the highest marks, so they're going to the competition. Good luck!' The day of the competition was here.

There were children from many different schools there. We all went into a big room with our teachers and listened carefully to the instructions. Then we were ready for our first test. We had to remember 35 words, and in the correct order.
(4) _____ 'Tony the Crocodile wears pyjamas when he plays board games in rockets to space with his vegetarian friends ...'

It was my turn. 'Crocodile, pyjamas, board games, rocket, space, vegetarian ...'

I got all 35 words right.

There were lots more tests I had to do. For example, I had to try and remember the names and faces of 40 people. I also had to remember a long list of numbers.
(5) _____ There were hundreds!

Unfortunately, I didn't win, but Mario and I both had a great time. When I saw Mr Holmes, he said 'Well done Clara! But you don't have an excuse for forgetting your homework now!'

A   Everyone found it very difficult.

B   I invented a silly song and sang it silently in my head.

C   Mario and I wrote an essay about the competition.

D   For each challenge, we had limited amounts of time to memorise everything.

E   We were all very excited when we heard this.

F   Emily and I talked about how we memorised these things.

G   I found drawing pictures for all the words was quite helpful.

H   Then Mr Holmes made the announcement we were all waiting for.

Grammar: past simple and present perfect time phrases

1 **Complete the sentences with the correct form of the verbs in brackets.**

1 We _____ Legoland last month and we went on all the rides. (visit)

2 I _____ just _____ the instructions, but I still can't make the robot. (read)

3 _____ you _____ your project on space yet? You have to hand it in today. (finish)

4 _____ you _____ a certificate for Man of the Match yesterday? (get)

5 Pedro _____ to Juan Pablo since the start of term, but I don't know why. (not speak)

2 **Match the sentence halves (1–6) to their endings (A–E).**

1 Junjie completed his homework

2 Danny joined the Manchester United youth team

3 Gael has never watched a match

4 Luciana has been upset about her marks

5 Gaspar hasn't commented on my photos

A since the end of term.

B at the Türk Telekom Stadium

C yet. Maybe he will later.

D six weeks ago.

E 30 seconds before the teacher came into the room.

3 **Read, circle and complete.**

1
Have you received a certificate for swimming? (How did you feel? What did you do after?)		
		when I was 7. Very happy! Hot chocolate to celebrate!

2
Have you helped a stranger? (Who was it? What did you do? How did you feel after?)		

3
Have you made something to wear? (What was it? What colour was it? Who was it for? Were you happy with it?)		

4
Have you watched a film in English? (What was the film? Was it interesting? Was it easy to understand?)		

5
Have you met a famous person? (Who was it? Where did you meet them? What were they like?)		

6
Have you visited a relative in a different city? (Who was the relative? Where do they live? What do you do there?)		

1 Order the letters and write the words.

idnfcntoe _confident_   suvoner _____

lideedgth _____   mlca _____

tediesnert _____   itedexc _____

drebo _____   deriwor _____

2 Use the words in Activity 1 to complete the sentences.

1 I wasn't ___bored___ at the castle, I was just _____ about falling. The tour guide's talk was very interesting.

2 I was _____ in the presentation for the first hour, but after that, I fell asleep. Sorry!

3 I know you're scared of water, but there's no reason to be _____. Just stay _____, breathe deeply and swim through the cave.

4 I was _____ when I heard that Eddie Redmayne was Newt Scamander in *Fantastic Beasts and Where to Find Them*. I'm _____ about the next film!

5 I'm usually very _____ about tests, but I don't think I did very well in our end of year maths test. Did I do enough revision?

3 🎧 4.12 Listen and number the pictures in order.

4 🎧 4.13 Listen again. Choose the best answer and give reasons.

1 Mrs Palmer is *nervous* / *calm*. _____

2 James is *bored* / *interested*. _____

3 Chloe is *excited* / *worried*. _____

★ Grammar: past perfect

1 **Complete the sentences with the past perfect.**

| tell   be   ~~never win~~   just lock   not speak   not visit |

1 I'd never won _____ a competition before, but I have now!
2 He _____ the door when the phone rang.
3 They _____ the castle before, but they'd read about it.
4 It _____ a cold, dark day and then the sun came out.
5 We _____ our aunt that we were scared of the dark, but she didn't believe us.
6 You _____ to the man with the tall black hat before today.

2 **Complete the text with the correct form of the verbs in brackets.**

I **(1)** 'd never been _____ (never / be) to London before, but our class was doing a history project last term and so we planned a day trip. Before we went, we **(2)** _____ (choose) which places to go to. Our teacher **(3)** _____ (check) the prices and times of the trains and we **(4)** _____ (make) a plan. I was so excited! Our first stop was the Tower of London. It was the place where prisoners were held if they **(5)** _____ (upset) the king or queen in the past. Sometimes though the prisoners **(6)** _____ (do) anything wrong: Queen Elizabeth I was put in prison because her sister, Queen Mary, thought Elizabeth **(7)** _____ (want) to be queen instead. It was an amazing trip.

Speaking

B1 Preliminary for Schools

3 **Watch Ezgi and Pablo doing Part 1 of a speaking test.** Number the expressions in order.

1 I'm sorry, could you say that again, please? ☐
2 Oh sorry, I don't understand. ☐
3 Could you repeat the question, please? ☐

4 **Now plan your answers to the questions.**

How much homework do you do at home?

Do you know a good way to organise your time?

What was your last school project?

SPEAKING TIP! To hear a question again, remember to ask politely for help. Don't just say 'What?'!

5 ▶ **Watch again and write.** What phrases can you use to ask for clarification?

1 _____
2 _____
3 _____

PRONUNCIATION TIP! When asking for clarification, stress the word you don't understand.

1 **Complete the graphic organizer about the story.**

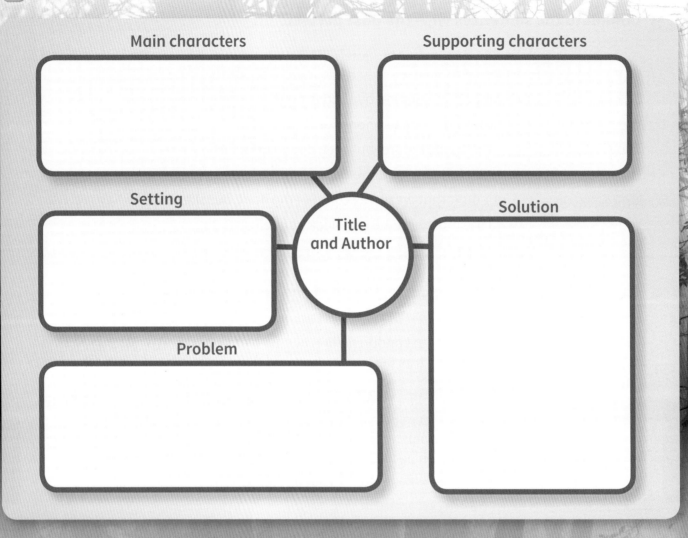

Main characters

Supporting characters

Setting

Title and Author

Solution

Problem

2 **Read and number the sentences in order.**

▢ They arrived very late at the campsite.

1 Joe and Natalia arranged a camping trip.

▢ Next day Sophie found the tent poles in the forest.

▢ They couldn't find the tent poles so they slept under the stars.

▢ Sophie didn't want to go camping.

▢ They all sat around the campfire and told scary stories.

3 **How do you think the bag of tent poles got into the forest?** **Write an explanation.**

_____

_____

_____

4 **Imagine you are sitting around the campfire.** **Which scary story would you tell?**

I would tell a story my uncle told me about a cyclist who disappeared …

5 🎧 4.14 ⭐ **Listen to six short conversations.** For each question, choose the correct answer.

1 Which place are they going to visit?

A ☐

B ☐

C ☐

2 What's the weather going to be like today?

A ☐

B ☐

C ☐

3 Who's the guide?

A ☐

B ☐

C ☐

4 What is the girl's favourite food?

A ☐

B ☐

C ☐

5 Where are the man's binoculars?

A ☐

B ☐

C ☐

6 What would the boy like to be when he's older?

A ☐

B ☐

C ☐

My progress: ☐ /6

1 Read the text again. Compare schools today to schools a hundred years ago.

A hundred years ago there were about sixty pupils in a
class. In my school there are twenty-five.

2 Ask a grown-up member of your family about their school. Write their answers.

1 Where did you go to school when you were my age?

2 How many children were in your class?

3 Were there boys and girls in your class?

4 What were your favourite subjects?

5 Did you use any type of technology in the class?

6 What didn't you like about your school? Why?

3 Write what you think schools will be like in 2117.

I think schools will

1 **For each question, choose the correct answer.**

The cleaner harbours project

Clean Harbours is a water project which started in 2014. The owner, Yannis Metaxis was anxious about the **(1)**… of pollution that he saw in the harbours when he went sailing. He felt extremely disappointed when he realised that some plant families had already disappeared. He has opened a learning centre next to the harbour and now he **(2)**… children and adults about the connection between water and the natural world.

School trips to this popular **(3)**… are mostly organised in the term time. As well as local plants, you can discover the life cycles and habitats of the **(4)**… marine life from the area.

Short courses are available for all ages and cover subjects such as recycling water or responsible tourism. Each course has a final test and in **(5)**…, you receive a certificate to show what you have learned. Yannis and his team are **(6)**… that the next generation will take more care of their environment.

1	A	amount	B	height	C	length	D	size
2	A	learns	B	studies	C	informs	D	involves
3	A	scenery	B	monument	C	entertainment	D	attraction
4	A	depressed	B	different	C	disappointing	D	difficult
5	A	case	B	reserve	C	addition	D	request
6	A	confident	B	helpful	C	reliable	D	calm

My progress: ____ /6

1 **Choose one of these questions.** Write your answer in about 100 words.

Part 2

Question 2

You see this notice on a school's website.

> **Articles wanted!**
>
> ## School Projects
>
> *What is the best subject for a school project?*
>
> *Is it one about the environment, the local town or the weather? Do you prefer to work on school projects alone or with a partner or in groups? Why? Give us your opinions.*
>
> **Write an article answering these questions and we will publish the best ones on our website.**

Write your article.

Question 3

- Your English teacher has asked you to write a story.
- Your story must begin with this sentence.

I read the instructions and felt confident. I decided to accept the challenge.

- Write your **story** in about **100** words.

My progress: ☐ /5

1 **Complete the sentences with the past simple or present perfect form of the verbs in brackets.**

1 I've been _____ to Florida lots of times, and I'm going again next year! (be)

2 We _____ calm when we went into the cave. We don't like dark spaces. (be)

3 _____ a comment on my photo late last night? (post)

4 Carmen and Samuel _____ the cake yet, but they made it yesterday. (decorate)

5 Anna _____ her leg skateboarding at the weekend. (break)

6 She _____ hockey for the school team since she was in Class 7. (play)

7 He _____ delighted about winning the maths competition. (look)

8 _____ the instructions correctly? We're on Step 4 now, but it doesn't look like a plane! (follow)

2 **Order the words to make sentences.**

1 because / disappointed / I was / really hard! / with my test mark / I'd tried

2 before / her. / the email / She / Tim phoned / hadn't read

3 his test / five more questions. / he turned the page / He'd finished / found / and then / and

4 the tickets / the car / They / when / were / they realised / 'd got in / on the kitchen table.

3 **Complete the sentences with the correct words.**

1 I'm not sure what to do next. An art c o u r s e or drama?

2 I know you're _____, but you could pretend to be interested in my lesson!

3 Yes, it's the last day of school. I know you're _____. I am too!

4 An _____ always has an introduction and a conclusion.

5 Don't worry. Stay _____ and you'll be fine!

6 The last day of the summer _____ is June 30th this year.

4 **Read the example.** Then, in pairs, discuss the other photos.

> The boy with number 27 on his shirt has won a competition and is delighted. The boy with number 9 on his shirt was confident and thought he had won.

6 Good job!

My goal

I can write an email stating preferences and making suggestions. **5**

Mission Complete!

I can take part in a conversation and use common expressions. **3**

I can order pictures to indicate a process. **4**

I can read and understand people's opinions on jobs and work. **2**

I can read and understand information on business cards. **1**

And I need ...

To do this, I will ...

So I can ...

I want to practise ...

Diary

What I already know about jobs and work ...

What I have learned about jobs and work ...

1 **Look and answer the questions.**

a sailor a politician ~~an architect~~ a hairdresser a musician a librarian a cleaner a scientist

1 Your parents have just bought this! Who should they phone first?

an architect

2 Lucia needs a haircut. Who should she see?

3 Ooooops! Somebody dropped a drink in the office kitchen. Who can help?

4 Who works here?

5 Who is going to come on stage?

6 What do you have to be to work here?

7 Who might tell them to be quiet?

8 Who speaks here?

2 **Read and write the jobs.**

1

Letters and parcels delivered every day in all weathers with a smile.

postman

2

I turn your brilliant ideas into the next bestseller. Call me! June

3

I design brilliant computer games. Check out my website to see what I can do!

4

Enormous houses | tiny apartments modern hospitals

No project too big or too small. Phone me to discuss

5

amy@amycutsforyou.com

Long, short, curly or straight,

The perfect style, just for you!

6

Dirty floors? Mess everywhere? Great!

Matthew – making all surfaces shine

3 **In pairs, say which three jobs you wouldn't like to do and why.**

I wouldn't like to be a scientist because …

1 🎧 4.15 **Listen and tick the correct sentences.**

1 The two women have met before. ✓

2 The man talks about three different books. ☐

3 The man and woman get on well. ☐

4 The woman is the Prime Minister. ☐

5 One of the men is 22. ☐

6 A musical instrument breaks. ☐

2 🎧 4.16 ⭐ **Listen again. For each question, choose the correct answer.**

1 What will Sarah's hair look like when she leaves the hairdresser's?

A ☐   B ☐   C ☐

2 Which is the best book cover for Tom's book?

A ☐   B ☐   C ☐

3 What's the woman's job?

A ☐   B ☐   C ☐

4 What's happening now?

A ☐   B ☐   C ☐

5 What job do the two speakers have?

A ☐   B ☐   C ☐

⭐ Grammar: modals of probability/deduction

1 Choose the correct answers to complete the sentences.

1 Tom **can't** / **might** be a librarian – he doesn't like reading!

2 Camila **must** / **might** be a musician. She can play the guitar well and I think she can sing.

3 It **could** / **must** be used for writing, but I'm not sure.

4 He **must** / **could** be a sailor. Only sailors are allowed on the boat.

5 Their new pet **can't** / **may** be a rat or it might be a cat. I didn't hear what they said.

2 Match the sentences (1–6) to photos (A–F). Then complete the sentences.

 A    **B**   **C**   **D**   **E**   **F**

A — 3

1 It _____ be angry, or it could be scared.

2 It _____ be a box, or it _____ be a glass cube. I'm very confused!

3 She __must__ be American. She has an American passport.

4 She _____ be on the tennis team today. She's got a broken leg!

5 It _____ be midnight. Happy New Year!

6 He _____ be at the hairdresser's. He hasn't much hair!

3 Read the notes and complete the sentences with *may, might, could, must* or *can't*.

Ben gets to school at 8:20.
The first bus leaves at 7:45.
The journey takes 35 minutes.
The first train leaves at 8:30.

Emilia hates cheese, but she loves potatoes. She can't eat tomatoes, but she doesn't mind onions, fish or pasta.

How does Ben get to school?

Ben **(1)** __may__ take the bus to school or he **(2)** _____ walk. He **(3)** _____ travel by train.

What is Emilia going to order?

She **(4)** _____ order tortilla, or she **(5)** _____ choose tuna with pasta. She **(6)** _____ order pizza because it has tomatoes and cheese.

4 Write sentences with *may, might, could, must* or *can't*.

The next President of the United States can't be Spanish.

_____

_____

_____

_____

_____

1 **Look at the code and write the words.**

♥a ▲e ◆i ■o ⬢u

1 ___■___ boss
2 ___■___ ___▲___♥___⬢___▲___
3 ___◆___
4 ___♥___ – ___◆___ ___▲___
5 ___♥___ ___♥___
6 ___♥___

7 ___▲___ ___◆___ ___▲___
8 ___⬢___ ___▲___ ___■___ ___▲___
9 ___♥___ ___▲___▲___
10 ▲___♥___
11 ___⬢___ ___–t◆___ ___▲___

2 **Complete the texts with the correct form of the words in Activity 1.**

If you want a (1) _career_ as a musician, you need to start when you're young. This is Alma Deutscher. She plays the piano and violin and writes and performs her own operas!

Hi Jenny,
Guess what? I've decided to (2) _____ my job! I don't really like my (3) _____ because she's always rude to me. Anyway, I've decided to leave to join the circus, or climb Mount Everest, or something! 😀
Speak soon,
Adrian

Next year I want to get a (4) _____ job, just at the weekends and during the school holidays. I don't mind what I do but if my (5) _____ are nice people, I'll be happy!

Kim,
Remember it's your dad's last day at work today before he (6) _____.
So, we're going out for a meal to celebrate. Don't forget!
Mum

Dear Aunt Fix-it,

I'm a bit worried about my sister Sofia. She's 21 and she's (7) _____ at the moment. She can't afford to go out much because she doesn't (8) _____ any money. She's applied for jobs but had no luck. She's very clever, she's great with people and she got excellent grades at university. What should she do next? Please help. Sam

I didn't spend much time with my parents when I was little because they set up their own travel business. Things improved after a few years and they employed some (9) _____. When I left school, I joined them too. I work (10) _____ and they pay me a good (11) _____. I work six days a week and enjoy every minute!

⭐ **Grammar:** present perfect continuous

1 Complete the sentences with the correct form of the verbs in brackets.

1 I've been studying programming at university for three months. (study)

2 _____ David _____ you in your new job? I asked him to this morning. (help)

3 She _____ at her desk today. I don't know where she is. (not sit)

4 Alp _____ as an architect for two years. She loves her job. (work)

5 Your colleagues _____ about you! They never talk about anyone. (not talk)

6 _____ you _____ for me for a long time? I'm so sorry I'm late. (wait)

2 In pairs, order the words to make sentences.

1 today / watching / Has / he / been / TV ?

2 been / a / reading about / We've / brilliant / Miley Cyrus. / article

3 been / you / Australia / How / travelling / have / long / around ?

4 been / their / doing / They / haven't / homework.

Speaking   ➤ **B1 Preliminary for Schools** ➤

3 ▶ Watch Ezgi doing Part 2 of a speaking test. Listen and number.

A OK `1`

B What else can I say? ☐

C … or something like that ☐

D I mean … ☐

E What's the word? ☐

F I guess. ☐

4 ▶ Watch again and say *yes* or *no*.

1 Ezgi starts by saying what job the man does.

2 She knows what the diagram is.

3 She mentions some equipment in the room.

4 She says what he looks like.

5 ▶ Imagine you're Pablo. Look at your photo. Describe it. Then listen to Pablo.

SPEAKING TIP! You can use small words like *OK* and *I mean* to give yourself more time to think.

6 ▶ Watch again and complete the sentences. Then ⟨circle⟩ the words that are stressed.

1 I _____ he _____ be an architect because it looks like a plan of a building on the whiteboard.

2 It _____ be the plan of an office or a hotel or _____ like that.

3 I think the other people in the room _____ be his colleagues.

4 It _____ like a good meeting.

1 **Answer the questions.**

1 Why was Mike alone in the house so often?
   Both his parents worked.

2 What was he working on at school?

3 Why does his project make him think about working now?

4 Was his father serious when he told Mike to start walking dogs?

5 How did Mike advertise his company?

6 Why has Mike stopped daydreaming?

2 **Imagine you were opening a dog walking company.** Write the information you would put on the internet.

The name of company

Your contact information

The time of day for walks and how long the walks are

What you charge

3 **Design a card for your company with your notes from Activity 2.**

4 ⭐ **Answer the question.** Write your answers in about 100 words. You are one of Mike's friends. Read the email and write back to Mike, using the notes you have made.

To:	Subject: Smart Dog Walking
From: Mike	
Hello everyone. I've started a company to walk dogs after school every afternoon. I now have so many dogs to walk that I need help. Would you like to work with me? You can walk dogs one at a time or several together. I'm planning to offer extra dog services for the clients' dogs. What sorts of things do you think I could offer? Of course we get paid for every dog we walk, so you'd earn some money. I hope you're interested in helping me. Mike	

Tell Mike

Tell Mike how many

Suggest something

Explain how much you want to earn.

Write your email to Mike using all the notes.

To:	Subject: Smart Dog Walking
From:	

1 **Look and write the correct word from the box and identify the economic sector they belong to.**

education   mining industry   farming   ~~health~~   food industry   construction

health

2 **Read and answer *yes* or *no*.**

1   Primary sector workers produce natural products or extract them from the ground.

2   Teachers and bus drivers work in the secondary sector.

3   Tertiary workers provide a service to customers.

4   The secondary sector uses materials from the primary sector.

5   The energy industry is part of the primary sector.

3 **Find out what we can make from these raw materials.**

wheat _____   cotton _____

olives _____   leather _____

milk _____   sand _____

strawberries _____   wood _____

4 **Order the pictures.** **Write a sentence about each step of the chain of production.**

1 _{4.17} **For each question, choose the correct answer.**

You will hear an interview with a young musician called Danny.

1 When he was at school, Danny particularly enjoyed
  - **A** playing music with his friends.
  - **B** having individual lessons.
  - **C** taking part in concerts.

2 Performing at parties helped Danny to
  - **A** earn some extra money.
  - **B** improve his song-writing skills.
  - **C** feel more confident about playing in public.

3 How does Danny now feel about his first online music video?
  - **A** impressed by the way he sang in it
  - **B** surprised by how quickly it became popular
  - **C** embarrassed by the number of mistakes in it

4 In making his latest album, Danny found it hard to decide
  - **A** what order the songs should be in.
  - **B** what style the music should be.
  - **C** what picture should go with it.

5 What did Danny think of the festival he attended recently?
  - **A** It had an interesting variety of bands.
  - **B** It offered great value for money.
  - **C** It was in a suitable location.

6 What does Danny plan to do next?
  - **A** develop a new skill
  - **B** move to a different country
  - **C** work more with other musicians

My progress: ☐ /6

1 **For each question, write the correct answer.** Write <u>one</u> word for each gap.

Being a postman

This job is quite hard even though it looks easy. I've learned a lot about neighbourhoods and pets **(1)**… the years! Cats are usually friendly but some dogs can be dangerous. The strangest animal I've seen at one **(2)**… the houses is a monkey in the front garden!

The first thing I do each day is sort the mail with my colleagues. After a short break, we each take our bag and start our route. I love being a postal worker because I get to be connected with **(3)**… public. As well, I deliver on foot, by bike or with a small van. I have **(4)**… be prepared for all kinds of weather. For example, **(5)**… it's very rainy, I need to be careful not to get the flu.

Modern changes have been improvements to the uniform and encouraging more female workers. I feel more comfortable in the new uniforms, expecially the summer one. Part-time or full-time training starts **(6)**… young as sixteen. I didn't start when I was sixteen, but only a couple of years older. This can lead to some interesting career opportunities in IT and Business.

1 ☐☐☐☐   3 ☐☐☐☐   5 ☐☐☐☐☐

2 ☐☐☐☐   4 ☐☐☐☐   6 ☐☐☐☐

My progress: ☐/6

1 Complete the text with *may*, *might*, *could*, *must* or *can't*. Use each verb only once. There is more than one possibility.

In this photo, there's a man in a blue suit and red tie who is talking. There are people on stage with him. I think they
(1) _____ be his colleagues. There's a flag and some red, white and blue balloons at the back of the photo, so I think they
(2) _____ be in the United States. He **(3)** _____ be a musician because he hasn't got an instrument and he isn't singing. I don't know his name, but he **(4)** _____ be a politician because he's talking to lots of people and he looks serious. He **(5)** _____ want to be the next President of the United States.

2 Complete the sentences with the correct form of the verbs in the box.

> paint   sunbathe   ~~look after~~   play   drive   cook

1 I'm really tired because I've been looking after our new puppy all day.
2 Toby _____ computer games all day.
3 Which car _____ today?
4 _____ Sofia _____ her bedroom this morning?
5 We _____ on the beach all day. We've been swimming in the sea.
6 Vincente _____ in the kitchen. He's been writing a vlog.

3 Read and complete the crossword.

Down

1 When somebody doesn't have a job, they are …
2 Someone who designs buildings is an …
4 When you stop working permanently, usually when you're in your sixties, you …

Across

3 Someone who decides which books are written is a …
5 Someone you work with is a …
6 Someone who sometimes works in a laboratory is a …

Crossword 1 Down: u n e m p l o y e d

4 What does the man in the photo do? Where does he work? Who does he work with?

I think he must be a …

Review ••• Units 4–6

1 **Complete the sentences with the correct form of the verbs in the box.**

> ~~throw away~~   show   phone   speak   wear   could / pass   read

1 I'll throw away your stuff if you leave it on the floor!
2 A boarding pass _____ at the door of a plane.
3 '_____ you _____ your Grandma recently?' 'Yes, I have. I _____ to her yesterday.'
4 We _____ a bestseller in class this week.
5 I was confident that he _____ the exam because he always works very hard.
6 It's definitely a bracelet. It _____ in Egypt.

2 👁 **Find the mistake in each sentence. Rewrite the sentences correctly.**

1 He was show where to put his luggage, then he said hello to everyone else.

   He was shown where to put his luggage, then he said hello to everyone else.

2 I was working as a tour guide since July last year and I love my job.

   _____

3 The pilot he is called Robert and he works full time.

   _____

4 We are saw our local politician in the village at the weekend.

   _____

5 I don't must take a taxi to the airport because my mum's going to drive me.

   _____

6 Next term, I'm going to take after the violin. I've always wanted to learn how to play it.

   _____

3 **Complete the definitions.**

1 A _certificate_ is something you receive when you've done well in a competition or passed an exam.
2 A _____ is someone whose job involves playing an instrument or singing.
3 A person is _____ if they can't wait for something to happen.
4 A _____ is someone who goes travelling around lots of places for a long period of time.
5 A _____ is someone who flies a plane.
6 A _____ is the person who is in charge at work.

1 **Read this email from your English-speaking friend, Jo.**

To:	
From:	Jo

Hi,

I'm so glad you're allowed to visit me this summer. You must be very excited!

I know it's your first time flying on your own, so try not to worry. Since it's a long flight, what are you going to take with you, so you aren't bored?

I've got to do a school project during the holiday. Will you have any homework?

Mum and I will pick you up from the airport. What activity would you like to do during your visit?

Don't forget your passport!

See you soon,

Jo

Yes – say what

Yes!

Tell Jo what

Tell Jo and suggest something.

2 **Read Jo's email. Answer *yes* or *no*.**

1 Jo is looking forward to your visit.

2 Jo might not have flown before.

3 Jo has a test to do during the holiday.

4 Jo tells you where to meet at the airport.

3 **Now answer the question in Activity 1 using all your notes.** Write your answer in about 100 words.

To:	
From:	

EXAM TIP! In this part of the exam, you need to include each response in your answer.

7 It's the law!

Mission Complete!

My goal

I can listen to conversations and identify the main idea. **5**

I can read and understand about fingerprints. **4**

I can understand a conversation with a partner and ask for their opinion. **3**

I can understand job definitions. **1**

I can read a text and answer questions on different laws. **2**

Diary

What I already know about the law …

What I have learned about the law …

And I need …

To do this, I will …

So I can …

I want to practise …

1 Read and label the items. Use the words in the box.

crime   criminal   reporter   article   ~~headline~~   cameraman   interview

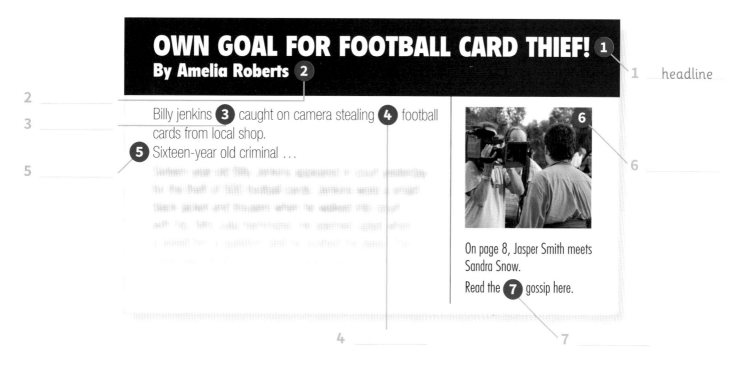

OWN GOAL FOR FOOTBALL CARD THIEF! 1
By Amelia Roberts 2

1 __headline__

Billy Jenkins **3** caught on camera stealing **4** football cards from local shop.
5 Sixteen-year old criminal . . .

On page 8, Jasper Smith meets Sandra Snow.
Read the **7** gossip here.

2 _____
3 _____
5 _____
6 _____
4 _____
7 _____

2 Read and complete the definitions.

1 A judge is someone who says what punishment a criminal receives.

2 A _____ is someone who goes to court with someone who has problems with the law and advises them.

3 A _____ is someone who investigates crimes.

4 A _____ is someone who breaks the law.

5 A _____ is someone who writes about the crime in an article.

6 A _____ is someone who films the criminal walking into court.

3 Complete the article.

Sixteen-year-old **(1)** __criminal__ Billy Jenkins appeared in court yesterday under arrest for the theft of 500 football cards. Jenkins wore a smart black jacket and trousers when he walked into court with his **(2)** _____, Mrs Julia Hammond. He seemed upset when a **(3)** _____ asked him a question, and he pushed the **(4)** _____ away. The judge said stealing from a shop was a serious **(5)** _____ and a serious punishment was the only option. Jenkins will spend 100 hours picking up litter from outside the local shops and parks. **(6)** _____ Ashton, who investigated the crime, said she was happy with the result.

For each question, choose the correct answer.

Police officer Simon, talks about his job.

I decided to become a police officer because I like the idea of helping people and making the world a safer and better place. Before I could go out in my uniform, I had to learn lots of laws that exist here in England. The majority of them are obvious – we all know that we aren't allowed to steal things, or drive too fast, or go through red traffic lights. But then I found some really unusual ones!

Imagine you're invited to a fancy-dress party while you're on holiday here in the UK. There are lots of people you could dress up as, but if you're caught wearing a sailor's uniform, you could go to jail for three months. So, you ought to bring something else to wear instead. While you're packing your luggage, it's useful to know that you can bring potatoes from anywhere in the world, just not Poland. You probably won't get through security at the airport if you have a few Polish potatoes in your bag. If you follow our laws, you won't get arrested and you'll have a great time and leave with happy memories. Don't even think about putting a stamp on a postcard upside down. It's against the law in the UK!

You might think our laws in England are a little odd, but then I spoke to a detective from Italy. In his country, you aren't allowed to build sandcastles on a particular beach or wear flip-flops if they're noisy. And if you see this headline 'Worker falls asleep in Cheese Factory', please don't laugh. It's a serious crime in Italy.

Of course, most of these strange laws are funny and you probably wouldn't go to jail if you broke them, but it's a good reminder that before we travel anywhere new, we should always read about how to behave so we don't get in trouble or upset people.

1   What does Simon say about most laws in the UK?

   A   There aren't many laws because it's a safe place.

   B   Most laws are about driving and traffic.

   C   Most laws are things that everybody knows.

   D   Only policemen understand them.

2   In the second paragraph, what is illegal in the UK?

   A   carrying potatoes from any countries in your bag

   B   wearing a police officer's uniform

   C   tearing a postcard

   D   putting a stamp on something the wrong way

3   What mustn't you do in Italy?

   A   wearing noisy footwear

   B   play sport on certain beach

   C   laugh at newspapers

   D   visit cheese factories

4   What would be a good introduction to this article?

   A   Policeman Simon Holmes tells us about some surprising rules around the world.

   B   In this article, Police Constable Simon Holmes talks about his experiences of being a policeman in different countries.

   C   After being a policeman in the UK for many years, Simon Holmes retires and investigates strange laws in other countries.

   D   For Police Constable Simon Holmes being a policeman is very boring. Here he tells us about his first year in the job.

★ Grammar: reported speech

1 **Look at the words in red. Choose the correct answers.**

1 "You're a criminal!" The judge said that I *(was)*/ *had been* a criminal.

2 "Chloe didn't go to school today." Sarah said that Chloe *didn't go* / *hadn't gone* to school *that* / *this* day.

3 "Javier has broken a window." Mum said that Javier *breaks* / *had broken* a window.

4 "I can play volleyball on this beach." Xiang said that he *is able to* / *could* play volleyball on *that* / *this* beach.

5 "We'll go to Brazil next year." Matteo and Diego said that they *would go* / *are going* to Brazil *that* / *the following* year.

6 "Mia and I must talk to Detective Fraser now." Mia said that she and Emma *must* / *had to* speak to Detective Fraser *then* / *now*.

2 🎧 **5.02** **Rewrite the sentences in reported speech.** Then listen and check your answers.

1 'I'm coming to your party tomorrow!' (Helen)

Helen said she was coming to my party the following day.

2 'I can't hang out with you today.' (Renata)

3 'You're talking to my sister.' (Ben)

4 'Aunt Sarah and Uncle James have arrived at our house.' (Mum)

3 **Read the messages from Sebi.** Complete the report in reported speech with 1–3 words in each gap.

10.20	I'm in the café with Mandy. We're sitting next to the window.
10.21	There are lots of people we know here.
10.27	We've got a great view of the street.
10.44	We can see two men on motorbikes.
10.45	There's a lot of noise. What should I do?
10.47	I'll call the police.

Earlier this morning, Sebi said he **(1)** ___was___ in the café with Mandy. **(2)** _____ at a table next to the window. **(3)** _____ lots of people **(4)** _____ . Apparently, they all **(5)** _____ something to eat or drink. At just before half past ten, Sebi said that they **(6)** _____ a good view of the street. Then at 10.44, Sebi sent another message. He said that he and Mandy **(7)** _____ two men on motorbikes. Just a minute later there **(8)** _____ a lot of noise and he asked what he **(9)** _____ do. Two minutes later he said he **(10)** _____ call the police. I wonder what happened next?

1 **Find six verbs in the wordsnake.**

interruptscreamwhispercomplainjokedemand

2 **Complete the sentences with the correct verbs in Activity 1.**

1 One girl is w h i s p e r i n g to her friend in class. Our teacher said that was very rude.

2 That ride looks very frightening. Did you _____ when you were upside down?

3 The footballer _____ to the referees about their decision. He thought it was unfair.

4 Sally's mother _____ about not having enough flour when there was flour everywhere!

5 Rafael _____ his father when he was working.

6 There are a lot of people in the streets. They're tired of things and are _____ change.

3 🎧 **Listen and complete the sentences with correct form of the verbs in the box.**
5.03

ask ~~reply~~ interrupt scream suggest demand complain whisper joke claim

1 David _asked_ Mia what she thought of the headline. Mia _replied_ that it was shocking.

2 Fiona _____ going to the cinema.

3 The librarian _____, 'Be quiet!'

4 Jessica _____ about her holiday.

5 Gabriel _____ that he had been best friends with George Ezra since school.

6 Jimena _____ that he had looked like a clown.

7 Juan Diego _____ another pizza immediately.

8 Emily _____ that there was a snake in her room.

9 Beth _____ the tour guide to ask about breakfast.

4 **In pairs, say and guess the verb.**

Emma ... that my dog had taken her sandwich.

Joked?

No, she wasn't laughing.

Screamed?

No, she wanted me to make her a new sandwich.

Ah, complained!

⭐ Grammar: reported questions

1 **Complete with the correct form of *ask* and the missing words.**

1 'When is your birthday?' She _asked when her_ birthday ___was___ .

2 'Are you American?' He _____ I _____ American.

3 'Will you visit the Great Wall in China?' They _____ I _____ the Great Wall in China.

4 'Can you bake cakes, Clara?' Maria _____ Clara _____ bake cakes.

5 'Has your sister done her homework?' Mum _____ sister _____ her homework.

6 'Do you play tennis?' He _____ I _____ tennis.

2 **Correct the mistakes in the sentences.**

1 Lucia asked me if I can help her with her project. _____

2 Yan asked Jing how old was she. _____

3 Tomas asked Francesca she was going on the school trip. _____

4 Beatrice asked Lucas if he did had a laptop. _____

5 Felipe asked Bruno when leaves the bus. _____

Speaking

B1 Preliminary for Schools ➤

4 **In pairs, discuss the situation below.**

A school has won £1000 to spend on anything you want.

SPEAKING TIP! In a conversation, we usually ask each other questions to get more information and to keep the conversation going.

5 **Watch again and <u>underline</u> where the stress falls.** Mark the direction of the intonation.

That would be OK, wouldn't it?
I don't think that would be a fun job.

3 📝 **Watch Ezgi and Pablo doing Part 3 of a speaking test. Tick the questions you hear.**

A What do you think of …? ☐

B Why do you think that? ☐

C That would be OK, wouldn't it? ☐

PRONUNCIATION TIP! Your feelings can affect how you express your opinion. When offering an opinion, think carefully about how strongly you want to express it.

1 **Answer the questions about the story.**

1 What did Robert McGinty do?

2 What is Elizabeth Sánchez' job?

3 Why was it hard to catch Robert McGinty?

4 Did Elizabeth Sánchez catch Robert McGinty on her own?

2 **Read the sentences. Do you agree with them? Why? Why not? Discuss your ideas in a group.**

1 Criminals like Robert McGinty should go to prison for a long time.

2 Criminals like Robert McGinty shouldn't go to prison. They should do work in the community to help other people.

3 Police officers should only try to catch criminals. It isn't their job to think about why people commit crimes.

4 We should help criminals change their behaviour.

3 **How can we keep safe online?** Write your ideas below.

4 **In pairs, discuss your ideas from Activity 3.**

FACT!

The world's first modern police force was London's Metropolitan Police Service. Set up in 1829 by a politician called Sir Robert Peel, the professional police officers who worked for the service became known as bobbies (Bobby is short for Robert). Some people in the UK still call police officers bobbies.

5 **Find out about the police force in your country.** Write four facts.

For each question, choose the correct answer. Write <u>one</u> word in each gap.

Write your answers in **CAPITAL LETTERS** below the text.

The day my identity was stolen

I'd just come home and turned my computer on. I was surprised to see a picture on the screen. It was of **(1)** .... foot above a banana skin. Under the image there was a message. 'Don't slip up,' **(2)** .... said.

When I realised that I couldn't delete the picture I felt angry. I turned my computer off **(3)** .... on, but the picture was still there. I couldn't use my computer.

(4) .... next day the bank told me there wasn't **(5)** .... money left in my account. I phoned the police. 'You're not the only one,' they said. 'Somebody's been stealing people's identities online.' I felt such a fool. It took six months **(6)** .... get my money back.

---

1 ☐☐☐☐☐

2 ☐☐☐☐☐

3 ☐☐☐☐☐

4 ☐☐☐☐☐

5 ☐☐☐☐☐

6 ☐☐☐☐

EXAM TIP! Think of the part of speech that needs to fill each gap. For example, does the gap need a pronoun (it, she), an article (the, a) or a preposition (of, in)?

1 **Read and answer the questions**

1 When do the lines on our fingers and thumbs form?

2 Explain how a fingerprint can identify a person.

3 When did the police first use a fingerprint to solve a crime?

4 Explain how technology can make police work easier.

5 What should you do if you do not want to leave fingerprints?

2 **Describe the fingerprints.** Find the two that are the same.

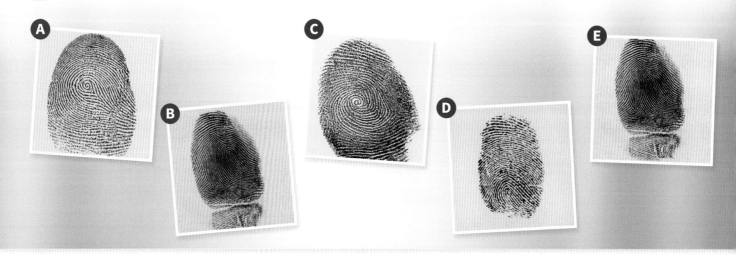

3 **Make a fingerprint.** In pairs, compare yours to your partner's.

Remember the words:

arches

loops

whorls

My fingerprints

_____

My partner's fingerprints

_____

My fingerprints have got …

4 **In pairs, read and answer the questions.**

1 What other ways can fingerprints be used for identification?

2 When will a fingerprint not help the police in their investigation?

3 Can you think of a material that will be difficult to find fingerprints on?

4 Why mustn't you touch anything at a crime scene?

Fingerprints can be used on identity cards and …

1 **For each question, choose the correct answer.**

Writer Ishmael Hanes talks about his work

I'm a crime writer and I get many of my ideas from real events. As you can imagine, reading the daily newspapers takes up most of my morning. If you read about the same thing in more than one newspaper you often get different points of view or you find out extra details, which I love searching for. For example, in one paper there was an article about a young woman who had complained about her neighbour's loud music. She said her terrible headaches were due to the noise. In another paper, the neighbour claimed that he didn't know the woman. When the reporter asked him what kind of music he liked, the neighbour replied that he hardly listened to music ever since he had an accident that had damaged his hearing.

More serious articles about thieves or break-ins are what I like reading about the most. My fans ask me, 'Don't you feel depressed if you read too many stories like that?' The honest answer is no! My imagination makes me think about all kinds of situations and my characters meet all kinds of people around the world.

When I was at secondary school, I always knew that I wanted to write and so my Literature teacher told me about an after-school writing club. I used to go once a week and it gave me a sense of what I wanted to do in the future. I wasn't very confident either, so meeting other young writers really helped me. We could try out ideas or discuss how our stories might end.

My parents didn't agree with my choice to become an author. They didn't believe I would earn enough in this kind of work. In fact, they wanted me to study Economics. Fortunately, my parents are proud of me now and I certainly don't have any regrets. I'm glad I went to university in the end because I made new friends and developed my abilities. I even won a prize for an interview with a lawyer which was published during my first year.

1 What does Ishmael say he enjoys most about reading newspapers?
   A using his mornings to only read articles
   B getting ideas for his work from articles
   C reading his favourite reporters' articles
   D noticing missing information in similar articles

2 What does Ishmael say about more serious articles?
   A They are what he prefers to read.
   B His fans don't like him reading those types of articles.
   C He creates characters from those types of crimes.
   D He is amazed when his readers solve the crimes.

3 Ishmael says that he joined a writing club
   A to help other young writers.
   B in order to please his teacher.
   C to practise writing stories.
   D to get some careers advice.

4 How does Ishmael feel now?
   A He is happy about his friendships.
   B He still wants to study Economics.
   C He is grateful for meeting a lawyer.
   D He regrets not earning enough money.

5 What would be the best introduction to this article?
   A For Ishmael, nothing is more important than his fans or winning prizes.
   B Ishmael describes how his ideas come from everyday stories in the papers and online.
   C In this article, Ishmael explains how he chose writing instead of Economics.
   D The man behind the popular detective books tells us about his interest in reading as well as his career choice.

My progress: ☐ /5

1 🎧 **For each question, choose the correct answer.**
5.04

1 You will hear two friends talking about a crime drama they watched on television.
    What did the girl find hard to understand?
    A   the way the story ended
    B   the reason why the crime took place
    C   the behaviour of one of the characters

2 You will hear two friends talking about jobs.
    What do they both think would be important for them in a job?
    A   getting on with colleagues
    B   being able to travel a lot
    C   earning a high salary

3 You will hear a boy telling his friend about a campsite he went to.
    How did he feel when he was there?
    A   annoyed by some of the other visitors
    B   disappointed with the weather
    C   surprised by how good the facilities were

4 You will hear two friends talking about a school project.
    What is the girl doing?
    A   offering to check what her friend has written
    B   explaining where her friend should look for information
    C   suggesting some ideas that her friend could use

5 You will hear a brother and sister talking about making a cake.
    What do they disagree about?
    A   when to do it
    B   what to put in it
    C   who to give it to

6 You will hear a brother and sister talking about
    a shoe shop they've just been to.
    The girl left the shop without buying
    anything because
    A   the assistants were unhelpful.
    B   the prices were too high.
    C   the shoes were the wrong size.

My progress: /6

1 Read and write the sentences in direct speech.

Someone took Mrs Stonesfield's favourite mug at lunchtime today. Who did it?

1   Robert said that he knew and would tell me what happened the next day.

'I know and I'll tell you what happened tomorrow.'

2   Rosie said that she couldn't be the culprit because she hadn't gone into Mrs Stonefield's classroom that day.

3   Hannah said that she had seen the mug there two hours before.

4   Jaime and Anna said that they were doing their homework then.

5   Mr Simpson said he didn't have his own mug and he borrowed a different mug every day.

2 Order the words to make sentences.

1   if I / Rebecca. / They / asked / called / me / was

2   to Mrs Greene / She / had / the problem. / asked / talked / she / Lucy / if / about

3   him / with / could / us / if / he / We / maths exercise. / help / asked / the

4   the music / Tim and Ben / No, turn / I / ask / could / didn't / if / they / off.

5   asked / had / school. / You / home / if / I / me / to / after / go

3 Order the letters and complete the sentences.

1   The **dlheneai** headline in the newspaper said 'Manchester United wins cup'.

2   The **veidecett** _____ **anddeedm** _____ to know the truth. The criminal refused to speak.

3   Jenny **pewderhis** _____ her answer in court. The judge told her to speak up.

4   The head **ortrerep** _____ **gessutedg** _____ I went to interview the pop star.

5   Timmy is always **tiintuperngr** _____ when his teacher is talking.

6   The **mlincria** _____ **gedrae** _____ with the policeman but he was still arrested for stealing.

4 Match the sentence halves (1–6) to their endings (A–F).

1   Nina claimed

2   We screamed

3   The judge said

4   My mum's a lawyer

5   I asked the cameraman

6   Martha and I replied

A   when James jumped out from behind the door.

B   she didn't know who committed the crime.

C   not to film the interview.

D   that we didn't know the answer.

E   it was a very serious crime.

F   and she helps people in court.

8 Fantastic flavours

Mission Complete!

I can talk about meals and dishes and express preferences. **5**

I can answer questions about how healthy food is. **3**

I can listen and complete a text with specific words. **4**

I can have a conversation and give an account of what was said. **2**

I can complete a word puzzle with visual prompts. **1**

And I need ...

To do this, I will ...

So I can ...

I want to practise ...

 **Diary**

What I already know about food and taste ...

What I have learned about food and taste ...

1 Find the words and label the pictures.

tuna

c	u	c	u	m	b	e	r
u	**r**	c	r	e	a	m	**a**
r	c	o	c	o	n	u	t
r	c	p	d	r	**e**	l	u
y	f	e	k	i	h	a	n
s	e	a	**t**	c	d	m	a
b	j	r	i	e	**t**	b	g
r	s	p	i	n	a	c	h

2 Find the bold letters and write the word. _____

3 Read the descriptions (1–5). Match to the photos (A–E) and complete the descriptions.

1   No, it isn't vegetarian. It's got lots of red, green and yellow peppers, but there's some ___tuna___ as well. And vegetarians don't eat fish. I think I'll have it for my first course. ☐

2   I choose this one. It's a delicious type of cake with fruit. Can you guess what the fruit is? It isn't apple, it's _____ . I always pour _____ on top. ☐

3   This is Chinese _____ and I always have it when I go to Chinese restaurants. Chicken soup first, then lots of meat, fish like cod and rice dishes with this on the side. ☐

4   I don't usually like _____ , but when I was in Thailand, I tried this! One of the main ingredients is _____ , a large white fruit with a shell. ☐

5   That looks nice! There are lots of ingredients and it's very colourful. What's that in the middle, next to the bread? Is it _____ with _____ on top? I think you can have it before your main course. ☐

A    B    C    D 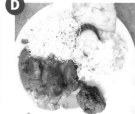   E

4 Look at Activity 3 again. In pairs, decide if the dishes are a starter, a main course or a dessert.

⟨ I think the dish of … ⟩

The young people below all want to go out for something to eat. Decide which location would be the most suitable for them. For questions 1-4, mark the correct letter (A-F).

1 Maria prefers eating at places that serve breakfast all day. She wants to try someplace that has recently opened and is popular with young people.

2 James wants to go out with his friends to a place known for its desserts. He'd like somewhere that has special offers and an international selection of desserts to choose from.

3 Niko would like to go out for dinner one evening with her college friends and do some activities while they're there. She'd also like someplace that offers discounts to students.

4 Michael is going on holiday to India with his family and would like to try a wide range of Indian dishes before he goes abroad. He'd like to find a special event where he can eat outdoors.

Reviews of the city's top places to eat

A
Door to India's food is amazing and their daily lunch special is one of the best in the city! You get to choose a delicious vegetarian curry with rice, and a soft drink for only £10 (£8 for students).

B
At the new Eat! festival you'll try food from around the world. Expect stalls to be selling anything from curries from India to ice cream from Italy. Entry is £2 or free for under 5s and students.

C
Sophie's Kitchen has won many awards for its huge range of delicious sweet dishes by using recipes from around the world. Be sure to download the app to book a table and get a free drink on your first visit.

D
Joe's is the new favourite place that college students are talking about. This restaurant breaks the rules by offering one menu absolutely full of tasty breakfast, lunch and dinner dishes served from 9am until midnight.

E
Come to 1Food for a food experience that you won't forget! Last year's annual international food festival had over fifty stalls selling Brazilian food in city square. At the same popular location, there'll be even more choice! This year's food sellers are going to be offering typical foods from India such as snacks, desserts and drinks.

F
Make sure you book to eat at Hot Spot or you won't get a table. This popular new restaurant offer's the city's tastiest selection of burgers with vegan, vegetarian and meat versions of every burger on the menu. There's an outdoor area to play pool or table tennis for a small fee or free with student ID. Open from noon till late.

⭐ Grammar: reflexive pronouns

1 Choose the correct answer to complete the sentences.

1 Did you hurt *yourself* / *herself* when you fell out of the tree?
2 Elena burned *itself* / *herself* on the pizza.
3 I taught *himself* / *myself* to cook.
4 Noa and Emma enjoyed *themselves* / *yourself* at the beach.
5 Ivan cut *ourselves* / *himself* on the steak knife.
6 You and Joel saw *themselves* / *yourselves* on TV after the concert.

2 Complete the sentences with the correct subject pronoun or reflexive pronoun.

1 Rachel and Becky, you saw yourselves in the newspaper at the weekend, didn't you?
2 I didn't blame _____ when the vase broke. It was an accident.
3 _____ have to behave yourself when you're in a restaurant, Gabriel.
4 Marta and Carla made _____ go jogging in the park every morning to get fit.
5 He didn't enjoy _____ last summer. It rained every day.
6 _____ surprised ourselves when our team came first in the competition.

3 Match the sentence halves (1–6) to their endings (A–F).

1 James wrote the   A themselves.
2 You cooked the   B ourselves.
3 I'm proud of myself for winning the   C letter himself.
4 We decorated the room   D pasta yourselves.
5 She made the   E art competition.
6 They tidied the garden   F bracelet herself.

4 First ask your friends or family about the following things. Then in pairs, ask and share information.

make a curry   bake a cake   change a lightbulb   do a PowerPoint presentation

Lisa, can you make a vegetable curry by yourself?

I'm not sure, I don't think so. I've never tried!

My sister Lucy can't make a vegetable curry by herself.

1 Order the letters to make food words.

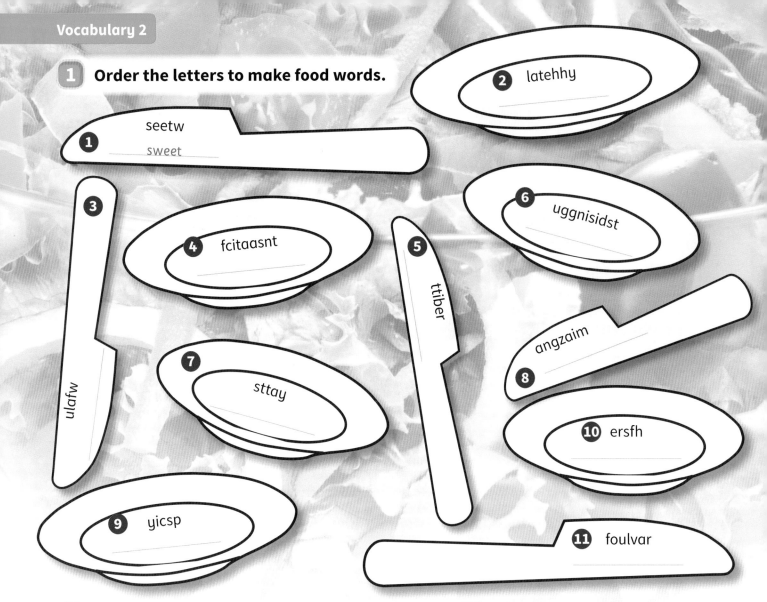

1 seetw
sweet

2 latehhy

3 ulafw

4 fcitaasnt

5 ttiber

6 uggnisidst

7 sttay

8 angzaim

9 yicsp

10 ersfh

11 foulvar

2 🎧 5.05 **Listen and number the pictures in order.**

A   B   C   D

3 🎧 5.06 **Listen again and write the words from Activity 1 in the correct column to describe the food in Activity 2.**

person 1	person 2	person 3	person 4

4 Choose the correct answer to complete the sentences.

1 The skin of a fruit like an orange is called *peel* / *top*.

2 The French word for 'candyfloss' means *grandad's* / *dad's* beard.

3 The peppers are called Aji peppers because that's the *look* / *sound* people make when they eat them.

4 The boy *can* / *can't* think of one positive things about his new diet.

⭐ Grammar: *too* and *enough*

1 Complete the sentences with *too*, *enough*, *for* and *to*.

1 Your dog is ugly, but it isn't ugly ___enough to___ win the World's Ugliest Dog competition.

2 It's _____ late _____ James _____ go out now. It's time for bed!

3 This tea is _____ sweet _____ drink. It's got 10 sugars in it!

4 Brilliant! It's now only £3. The T-shirt is cheap _____ me _____ buy!

5 Chocolate and sweets aren't healthy _____ you _____ eat for lunch at school.

6 Nina doesn't like her pink shoes now. They're _____ small _____ her _____ wear to school.

2 Complete the sentences with *too*, *enough*, *for* and *to*.

 **1** The pencils are _____ big for them _____ use.

 **2** She isn't well _____ go out.

 **3** The lemons are _____ bitter for them _____ eat.

Speaking 🎤

B1 Preliminary for Schools ➡

 3 ▶ **Watch Pablo and Ezgi doing Part 4 of a speaking test.**

Tick the things that Ezgi talks about:

how often she eats out with her family ☐

where her grandparents live ☐

how many cousins she has ☐

what type of fish she eats ☐

what vegetables she eats ☐

what she enjoys cooking ☐

> **SPEAKING TIP!** Answer the questions with as much information as possible, but don't speak for too long if the examiner wants to ask you another question!

 4 📝 **Now plan your answers to the questions.**

Do you like going out for meals?

Who do you like going out with?

Where do you go?

What type of food do you like?

 5 ▶ **Watch again and ⟨circle⟩ where the stress falls in each question.**

1 Do you like going out for meals?

2 Who do you like going out with?

3 Where do you go?

4 What type of food do you like?

> **PRONUNCIATION TIP!** When talking about things we like, our voice is light and positive. When talking about things we dislike, our voice is flatter and more miserable.

1 **Match the people to the planets.**

1   Lisa   2   Nurse   3   Tilly   4   Temoc

2 **Read the text again.** Answer the questions.

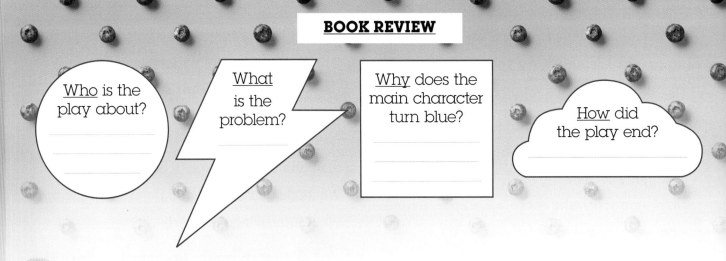

BOOK REVIEW

Who is the play about?
_____
_____

What is the problem?
_____

Why does the main character turn blue?
_____
_____

How did the play end?
_____

3 **Read and complete the text.**

The play is about a young girl called _____ Lisa _____

One day she asks her grandfather how to improve her brain power because
_____ and the school _____ .

Her grandfather says that when he was a boy they said you should eat lot of
_____ to improve your brain power.

This gives her an idea and she eats lots of _____ and
_____ .

Unfortunately, she _____ .

At the end of the play she _____ and isn't sent back to Earth.

8

4 ⭐ **Read the text below and choose the correct word for each space.**

Fun facts about food

1 Cutting onions releases a gas … makes you cry.

2 Ketchup was … in the 1830's as a medicine.

3 The fear of vegetables … called Lachanophobia.

4 The word vegetable has no scientific definition, … you can call a tomato a vegetable.

5 … a lot of beetroot turns your tongue a pink colour.

6 The first … was made from hippopotamus.

7 French fries came from Belgium but are … popular in the US.

	A	B	C	D
1	who	which	whose	when
2	drunk	eaten	made	used
3	were	are	is	was
4	so	that	but	and
5	Eat	Eaten	To eat	Eating
6	soup	snack	salad	dessert
7	a lot	more	many	much

1 **Answer the questions.**

1   What is a healthy diet?

2   Why should we read the labels on prepared food?

3   How much salt is unhealthy?

4   What happens if we eat too much sugar?

5   Why are additives put into food?

2 **Do you always know what you are eating?** Are you sure?
**Read the ingredients in the bar of chocolate. Can you find
the surprise ingredient?**

The surprise ingredient is _____ .

3 **Read the food labels of three different food products
at home.** Answer the questions.

Which one contains

1   the most sugar?   _____

2   the most fat?   _____

3   the most salt and sodium?   _____

4   Do any of the food products contain too much sugar, fat, salt or sodium?   _____

4 **Complete the table with food or meals that contain these ingredients.**

Milk	Cheese, cake, chocolate
Eggs	
Wheat	
Nuts	
Fish	
Seafood	

Did you know?

A food allergy is a medical condition that causes you to have a bad reaction to something you eat. The most common food allergies and intolerances are caused by: milk, eggs, wheat, nuts, fish and seafood. Food additives can also cause allergies.

1 🎧 **5.07** **For each question, write the correct answer in the gap.** Write one or two words or a number or a date or a time.

You will hear a man called Rik Price telling a group of young tourists about his work.

Owner of a farm

Rik never has to wear a **(1)** .... when he's working.

Rik got some more **(2)** .... about two years ago.

Rik says that today's menu for the visitors is rice, a **(3)** .... and a fruit salad.

Rik is very proud of the **(4)** .... that he recently started growing.

Last year **(5)** .... destroyed all of Rik's peppers.

In next year's 'Small Farms' competition, Rik will need to show how much **(6)** ...... the farm does.

My progress: ⬜ /6

Work in groups of three: one examiner and two candidates, A and B.

A and B: listen to the examiner and speak together for 2–3 minutes.

Examiner: ask questions to A <u>or</u> B.

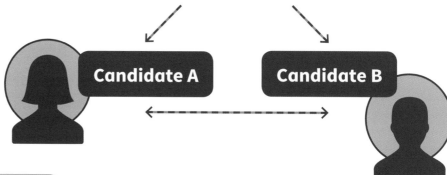

Examiner

Candidate A   **Candidate B**

What's your favourite healthy meal? (Why/Why not?)

Who do you like going to restaurants with?

Do you like trying new food when you go on holiday? (Why/Why not?)

What special dishes do you have in your country?

Do you prefer watching cooking programmes or food documentaries on TV?

Thank you. That is the end of the test.

My progress:		
I understood and answered all the questions. ☐	I understood and answered most of the questions. ☐	I didn't understand all the questions and needed some help. ☐

1 Complete the sentences with the correct reflexive pronouns.

Fiona What did you do last night, Martin?

Martin Andy came to my house and we cooked pizza **(1)** _ourselves_.

Fiona That sounds fun.

Martin Well, no, not really. When I was chopping the onion, I cut **(2)** _____ on a knife.

Fiona Oh dear. What did Andy do?

Martin Well, he ran to get a bandage but fell over his shoes.

Fiona Did he hurt **(3)** _____ badly?

Martin Yes, he did. We had to go to hospital.

Fiona So you didn't enjoy **(4)** _____ last night?

Martin Not really, no. And I'm not going to cook pizza **(5)** _____ again.

2 Match the sentence halves (1–6) to their endings (A–F).

1 You aren't old enough

2 It's too cold for him

3 The bike is too expensive for him

4 Is the lemon cake easy enough for him

5 Are you tired enough

6 The joke is too silly

A to buy.

B to walk to the market by yourself.

C to repeat!

D to go to bed before dinner?

E to go out without a hat and scarf.

F to make himself?

3 Complete the sentences with the words in the box.

> dessert   coconut   ~~starter~~   amazing   spinach   vegetarian   spicy   fantastic   main course

When I go out for meals, I always make sure I don't eat too much for the **(1)** _starter_ or **(2)** _____ because I want to be able to eat **(3)** _____. For me, it's the best part of the meal. I went to a really nice Indian restaurant last weekend for my mum's 40th birthday. They made my mum a special **(4)** _____ cake which I had with ice cream. I'd never tried it before, but it was **(5)** _____.

The rest of the meal was **(6)** _____ too. I don't eat meat or fish so I always have **(7)** _____ food. We all shared lots of dishes. My favourite was a vegetable curry. It was very hot and **(8)** _____. When we left the restaurant my brother said 'Aynur, what have you got between your teeth?' When we looked at the photos of my mum's birthday the next day, there was me smiling with **(9)** _____ between my teeth.

4 In pairs, answer the questions.

1 Think of something you couldn't eat. What was the problem and what happened?

2 Do you like spicy food? Why? / Why not?

3 What aren't you old enough to do yet?

4 What are you too big to do?

> The last thing I really couldn't eat was …

9 Raining cats and dogs

I can write an article about a restaurant. **5**

Mission Complete!

I can tell a story using visual aids. **3**

I can read and understand a text about tornadoes. **4**

I can identify different topics in conversations. **2**

I can read sentences about about the Earth and say if they are true or false. **1**

My goal

And I need …

To do this, I will …

So I can …

I want to practise …

Diary

What I already know about the weather …

What I have learned about the weather …

9

1 Complete the texts with weather words.

Come to sunny Mexico in August!
With 11 hours of **(1)** sunshine a day,
(2) t_____
between 25 and 34 **(3)** d_____
centigrade and hardly any
(4) s_____, it's the perfect holiday
destination! Go online to download our brochure.

Michael Fish presented a
(5) w_____ f_____ in 1987
and told people not to worry about a
(6) s_____. The next day, the worst
one for three centuries hit the South of
England!

Both animals and humans can
suffer from astraphobia, a fear
of **(9)** t_____ and
(10) l_____ .

FACT FILE

When you think of Australia,
you usually think of extreme
(7) h_____ and barbecues
on the beach. But in 1900,
Australia had its heaviest ever
(8) s_____. In
some places it was 50 cm deep!

This is the Beaufort scale, which is used to
measure wind speed (in kilometres per hour)

2	3	4	5	6	7	8	9
light **(11)** b _ _ _ _ _	gentle	moderate	fresh	strong	near **(12)** g_ _ _		strong
6–11	12–19	20–28	29–38	39–49	50–61	62–74	75–88

2 Complete the table with what people can do in the weather conditions.

🙂		🙁
	sunshine	
	showers	
	storm	
	snowfall	
	thunder	
	lightning	

3 In pairs, talk about your town. Say what you can do in different types of weather.

⤶ When it rains, you can go to …

Welcome to my town!

The weather is usually
great here, but don't
worry if it rains. Here
is our new 10-screen
cinema. All the newest
films are shown here
and the popcorn is
delicious! It's perfect for
when there are showers.

1 🎧 5.08 **Listen and circle the words that you don't hear.**

1   doctor   problem   (snowy)   old
2   four   kilometre   seconds   crisp
3   unusual   dark   lucky   tennis
4   rock   windy   cottage   mountains
5   forecast   heavy   thunder   dangerous
6   beach   water   strong   huge

2 🎧 5.09 ⭐ **Listen again. For each question, choose the correct answer.**

1   You will hear a brother and sister talking about their grandfather.

What do they say about him?

A   He's good at making people laugh.

B   He has certain health problems.

C   He always behaves in the same way.

2   You will hear two friends talking about a storm.

How does the girl feel?

A   unsure whether to trust her friend

B   anxious about what might happen

C   embarrassed by her lack of knowledge

3   You will hear a girl talking to her friend about her day yesterday.

What was she upset about?

A   not having the time to do everything she wanted

B   not feeling warm enough to go out

C   not being able to do what she'd planned

4   You will hear a girl telling a friend about a holiday she had in Scotland.

What surprised her about the place she went to?

A   how much the weather changed

B   how friendly the local people were

C   how beautiful the landscape was

5   You will hear a mother and her son talking about the weather tomorrow.

The boy thinks his mother

A   worries too much.

B   needs to be careful.

C   has the wrong information.

6   You will hear a brother and sister talking about a video they are watching.

They agree that the man in the video

A   is doing something dangerous.

B   is amusing to look at.

C   is familiar to them.

⭐ Grammar: review first and second conditionals

1 **Choose the correct words to complete the sentences. Then** (circle) **1ˢᵗ or 2ⁿᵈ conditional.**

1 We *don't* / (*wouldn't*) wear scarves if it was 40°C!   **1ˢᵗ /** (**2ⁿᵈ**)

2 If you *take* / *took* your umbrella, you won't get wet.   **1ˢᵗ / 2ⁿᵈ**

3 I *am* / *'ll be* amazed if there's snowfall in July.   **1ˢᵗ / 2ⁿᵈ**

4 *Would* / *Will* they scream if they hear thunder?   **1ˢᵗ / 2ⁿᵈ**

5 If a snowman *can* / *could* speak, I'd be surprised!   **1ˢᵗ / 2ⁿᵈ**

6 If you *made* / *make* a mistake, would you tell me?   **1ˢᵗ / 2ⁿᵈ**

2 **Match the sentence halves (1–8) to their endings (A–H).**

1 If you forget your homework,   A they wouldn't wear them in the snow.

2 If Sophia and Aria had new shoes   B you would tell everyone!

3 If Rafael was sad,   C I wouldn't buy him another present.

4 If you don't wear sunglasses,   D he would talk to Amy.

5 If Sam is on holiday,   E Mrs Wang won't be happy.

6 If Marta told you a secret,   F your eyes will hurt.

7 If you swim in the sea in January,   G you'll freeze!

8 If James didn't say thank you,   H he won't come to your party.

3 **Write complete sentences.**

1 I / not phone Grandma / she / be upset _____

2 Dad / fly to Berlin / they / not cancel the plane. _____

3 your bike / be better / you / enter the cycling race _____

4 they / eat ice cream / it / not snowing _____

4 **In pairs, look and complete the sentences.**

If he doesn't eat his vegetables, he'll …

1 If he doesn't eat his vegetables, …

2 … if he doesn't score a goal.

3 If I met a dog that could dance, …

4 … if my parents owned a sweet shop.

1 **Look and write the complete word.**

1 ☐y☐i☐a☐ _typical_
2 c☐☐o☐ _____
3 ☐a☐m _____
4 h☐m☐d _____
5 ☐e☐ _____

6 m☐☐l☐ _____
7 ☐r☐e☐i☐g _____
8 s☐o☐y _____
9 ☐☐c☐ _____
10 d☐y _____

2 **Order the words from hot to cold.**

cool   warm   mild   freezing

_____   _____

3 🎧 5.10 **Do the quiz.** Answer *yes* or *no*. Then listen and check your answers.

1 The most humid places on Earth, like Kuala Lumpur and Hong Kong, are furthest from the Equator. _____

2 Due to global warming, the mountains in the Alps aren't as snowy now so ski resorts are using helicopters to drop white powder that looks like snow! _____

3 The wettest place on Earth is Mawsynram in India. In a typical year, there is 11.87 metres of rainfall. So, imagine you have six tall basketball players and they stand on each other's shoulders, the water would cover their heads! _____

4 This is a Beluga whale. It is the only whale that stays in the Arctic when the icy water freezes. _____

5 Antofagasta in Chile, which is the driest place on Earth, only gets 1mm of rain a year! _____

4 📋 **Find three interesting weather facts and write a quiz.**

⭐ Grammar: *I wish...*

1 **Complete the sentences with *wish* and the correct form of the verb below.**

> ~~be~~   not have to go   let   not live   have   can

1   I _wish_ it _was_ summer.
2   We _____ our dad _____ in Antarctica.
3   Ahmet and Esma _____ their mum _____ them go to bed later.

4   You _____ you _____ to the dentist today.
5   James _____ he _____ a brother.
6   The cat _____ it _____ fly.

2 **Complete the sentences about the pictures.**

1   Hannah _____ a camel (can ride)
2   Alvaro and Diego _____ superheroes. (be)
3   Ben _____ correct answer. (know)

Speaking   ▶ **B1 Preliminary for Schools**

3 ▶ **Watch Pablo and Ezgi doing Parts 3 and 4 of a speaking test. Circle the topics they talk about.**

weather   **films**   **the beach**   **dinosaurs**   **buildings**   **food**   **clothes**   **sport**   **shopping**

4 📝 **Discuss the pictures in Part 3. Then plan your answers to the questions in Part 4.**

1   Have you ever been to a different city in winter?
2   What do you think students would like to do in your city?

5 ▶ **Watch again and write the tag questions you hear.**

1   There are lots of things to do in capital cities, _____ _____?
2   It looks fun, _____ ?
3   It looks cold, _____ ?

> **SPEAKING TIP!**
> When you're talking about a photo, try to think of useful ideas and vocabulary about the topic.

PRONUNCIATION TIP! Try to make your voice go down at the end of a tag question.

1 **Number the pictures in order.**

2 **In pairs, tell the story from the pictures.** | The three friends wanted to enter the …

3 **Read the story again and complete the sentences.**

1 At first, Mitzi wanted to take _____ photos of people working. _____

2 In the end, they all decided _____.

3 On Friday, James checked _____.

4 Kevin didn't think _____.

5 When they reached the hills, they saw _____.

6 An hour after they started climbing, it _____.

7 They had to climb up to the top of the hill to _____.

8 The police sent _____.

9 Mitzi took a photo of the helicopter and _____.

4 ⭐ **Mitzi, James and Kevin are looking for new after-school activities.** Below there are descriptions of six different after-school clubs for young people. Decide which club would be the most suitable for each child.

James enjoys being out in the fresh air and he loves nature. He's interested in joining a group of young people who like being outdoors, too. He's keen on being active.

Mitzi loves being in the water so she'd like to find somewhere she can swim. She is not very competitive and is not interested in getting onto a team. She's also keen to meet new people and have fun.

Kevin loves being out and about on his bicycle. He dreams of being a competitive cyclist one day and would love to train to be the best. He loves being a member of a team and he loves winning!

A   Nature Trail

This is the ideal place to increase your knowledge of local flora and fauna! We have daily talks and seminars from experts in the field. Once a month, we organize a walk out into the countryside, so you can test your new knowledge.

B   Free-Wheeling

This club gives young people the opportunity to be great cyclists. Learn all the best techniques from other members and share your rides with them. It's all great fun! We have a gym to help you get fit!

C   Keep Active

This is the club to join if you love sports. We have cycling, tennis, soccer, volleyball, windsurfing and swimming. We organize competitions in all our sports. Try out for the different teams and meet our expert coaches.

D   Youth Club

This is a great club for youngsters who enjoy sports like tennis, soccer and swimming, but are also interested in meeting people of their own age and in enjoying social activities like a once-a-week disco.

E   All Sports

What are your favorite sports? Cycling, soccer, table tennis, basketball?

This is a club where you can watch your favorite sports on the large screen. We also have a variety of video games with the theme of sports. Enjoy our social programme which includes parties and dancing.

F   Out And About

This club is perfect for those who love the outdoors. We organize day-long walks out in the hills and enjoy nature. Meet people of your age with the same interests, and keep fit!

1 **Read the text about tornadoes.**

Tornadoes form over land. They form when air masses with a big temperature difference meet. The colder air pushes up the warm air very quickly and this causes the air to start spinning. It forms a dark spinning column that can travel across the land at 800 kilometres per hour. Tornadoes are sometimes called twisters because of the way they move. They look like big, black thunderclouds with a tail but they are much more dangerous than a thunder storm. When the tornado touches the ground, it can destroy everything in its path. It can pull up trees and throw buildings up into the air. It is like an enormous vacuum cleaner! Tornadoes are also very noisy. When they hit the ground, the noise can be as loud as a jumbo jet. Although tornadoes are very dangerous, some people chase them in their cars and try to drive through them for fun. They are called Tornado Chasers.

2 **Complete the chart about tornadoes.**

	Tornadoes
Where do they form?	
Why do they form?	
How fast can they move?	
What are their consequences?	
Why do some people go into them?	

3 **Find out information about a recent hurricane.**

1 What was its name?

2 When did it happen?

3 Which countries did it affect?

4 How many days did it last?

5 What were the consequences of this hurricane?

4 **In pairs, discuss what people need after a disaster?**

Think about:
- Housing
- Health
- Food
- Water
- Energy

> The people will need a place to stay and to be safe if they have lost their houses. They will also need …

1 **Read this email from your English-speaking friend Trea, and the notes you have made.**

To:	
From:	Trea

Hi,

You'll never believe it! I've won two tickets to attend the skiing championships on Saturday! Would you like to go with my family and me? —————————————————————— Yes, please

The event starts at 10am, so we'll need to leave quite early. Can you get to my house by 8 am or do you want us to pick you up on the —— Say which way to the ski resort? you prefer

After the ski event, we can do a winter sport! Would you prefer to go snowboarding or ice skating? —————————————————— Explain

We're going to be outside most of the day, so don't forget to wear really warm clothes. I've got lots if winter clothes. Do you need to borrow anything? ——

See you! ———— Ask to borrow!

Trea

Write your answer to Trea in about 100 words, using all the notes.

To:	
From:	

My progress: ☐ /5

Work in groups of three: one examiner and two candidates, A and B.

Examiner

 A and B: close your books. Listen to the examiner and speak together for 2–3 minutes.

 **Candidate A**   **Candidate B**

Examiner: read and then listen to A and B speak. Use a timer.

> Now, in this part of the test you're going to talk about something together for about two mintes. I'm going to describe a situation to you.

Show A and B the photos

> A teacher is talking to her students about a place for their school party. Here are some places they could go to. Talk together about the different places they could go to, and say which would be best. All right? Now, talk together.

> Thank you. (Can I have the booklet please?)

My progress:		
I understood and answered all the questions. ☐	I understood and answered most of the questions. ☐	I didn't understand all the questions and needed some help. ☐

1 Order the words to make sentences.

1 I / a / If / amazed. / met / be / real / I / would / unicorn

   If I met a real unicorn, I would be amazed.

2 get / flip-flops / If / feet / she / wet. / will / wears / her

3 I / you / my / pop / If / you. / won't / balloon / forgive

4 ice skating. / icy / it / If / so / we / go / wasn't / wouldn't

5 ill? / strawberries / be / we / we / these / If / will / eat

6 a / you / you / outside / do? / would / during lightning storm / what / If / were

2 Read the sentences. Write the wishes.

1 My mum and dad are in Berlin.

   I wish my mum and dad weren't in Berlin.

2 James isn't good at tennis.

3 Lucy doesn't have any headphones.

4 Carolina and Camila's little sister takes their clothes.

5 We don't live in a tent.

6 I can't sing well.

3 The words in bold are in the wrong sentences. Rewrite the sentences with the correct word.

1 When there's **weather forecast**, we always go to the seaside.

2 You shouldn't stand under a tree when there's **sunshine** and lightning.

3 I watched the **thunder** last night and it wasn't good news.

4 It isn't hot and **mild** here, it's just dry.

5 Unfortunately, this is **humid** winter weather for Scotland.

6 It isn't too hot and it isn't too cold. It's nice and **typical** at this time of year.

4 Look at the situations. What do you wish? Write sentences.

1 Your train is five hours late and it's raining.

2 You're hungry and you don't have anything to eat.

3 Your friend has a new pet and you want one too.

4 Tyler eats my sweets but doesn't ask first.

Review • • • Units 7–9

1 Choose the correct answers to complete the sentences.

1 Beth asked Taylor if she *was* / *had been* American.

2 I wouldn't ask my sister to cut my hair if she *hadn't been* / *wasn't* a hairdresser.

3 Georgia hurt *her* / *herself* when she fell on the ice.

4 Daniel and Sara said that their starters *were* / *are* disappointing.

5 It wasn't good *enough for* / *enough to* win the competition.

6 I wish I *were* / *am* a scientist.

2 Complete the sentences with the correct words.

1 They asked me if I __would__ take a photo of them.

2 I enjoyed _____ at your party last weekend, Tomas.

3 The judge said that it _____ been an easy decision. Both sides argued the case well.

4 Ben wishes he _____ have a broken leg. He wants to play football.

3 ⊙ Find the mistake in each sentence. Rewrite the sentences correctly.

1 You complained about that restaurant lots of times before.

   You have complained about that restaurant lots of times before. _____

2 Camila asked me how old am I.

   _____

3 If you didn't have your racket, you won't play tennis today.

   _____

4 If you'll speak to the detective, he'll ask you lots of questions.

   _____

5 I told Hannah if she was on the basketball team.

   _____

6 I wish my mum doesn't work on Christmas day.

   _____

4 Complete the sentences with the correct words.

1 It was very __icy__ this morning and I slipped and fell on the pavement.

2 The girls in my class were _____ because they didn't want anyone to hear.

3 _____ are long and green. They're tasty in salads or sandwiches with tuna or salmon.

4 There was 10 centimetres of _____ last night. Lots of the schools where I live are closed today.

1 **Look at the notice below.** Think about your article.

Articles wanted!

Awesome restaurants

What makes an awesome restaurant?

Is it the type of food, the staff, the decoration – or all of these things?

How important is it to have a choice of healthy food on the menu?

Tell us what you think!

2 **Read Lei's article.** Then (circle) six expressions used to express opinions or give examples.

(For me), an awesome restaurant is one that gives a warm welcome to everyone in the family. The waiters should be friendly to everyone, I also like it when they're funny. In my opinion, a restaurant doesn't need to have lots of types of dishes on the menu, for example, you can't expect paella in a Chinese restaurant even if it is your favourite meal, but the food should be delicious. As for the atmosphere, it's important that everyone's having fun. In my view, it's good if there's a choice of healthy food on the menu, but I eat healthy food at home every day, so I don't think it matters eating things like cake and ice cream instead of fruit occasionally.

3 **Now answer the question in Activity 1.** Write your article in about 100 words.

EXAM TIP!
You must give good examples to persuade the reader to agree with you.

6

POWER UP

Home Booklet

Paul Drury

With Caroline Nixon and Michael Tomlinson

MUSIC WITH NO MUSIC?

What type of music do you like: a bit of pop, some rap, maybe a bit of classical? Whatever type of music you like, it makes you feel a certain way. If you're sad perhaps you like to listen to sad music. If you're happy, you listen to happy music. But how would you feel about going to a concert and listening to ... nothing, no instruments, no singing, just silence?

This is exactly what the composer John Cage did in 1952. He asked a pianist to go onstage, sit at the piano, raise his hand and do absolutely nothing. The pianist didn't sing, he didn't dance, he didn't talk, he didn't play a single note. He just sat at the piano.

Why did he do it?

Cage was very serious about his work; it certainly wasn't a joke. Although the piece is often called *Silence*, Cage believed that silence didn't exist, there was always something to listen to. He also believed that any sound could be music. He wanted us to pay more attention to the sounds and noises around us.

Why don't you try it?

Sit somewhere comfortable, somewhere that is a little bit dark, set your stopwatch for one minute (or longer if you can). Get ready and be patient. Close your eyes, open your ears and just listen. Make a note of everything you hear. How does it make you feel?

Do you think it's strange? So do I. But it's an interesting idea, isn't it?

⭐ Home mission

It can be very difficult to find music that everyone likes. Copy the table below into your notebook and try and find one piece of music that everyone in your family likes. Do you dance to this music?

Name	Style of music	Do you like it?	Name one song/piece of music in this style that you like.
	Classical music		
	Pop music		

WINDOW TO THE WORLD

Japan is famous for many things and for being a very modern society but have you ever heard of Kabuki? This is a kind of opera that can last for around nine hours. You're not excited about the idea? Perhaps nine hours is a bit long but you can buy tickets for shorter parts of the performance. It's an amazing experience. It's part play, part theatre, part opera. The costumes are incredible and the actors are very well trained. Sometimes the audience calls out the name of the actor. This isn't rude; it's part of the tradition.

Would you like to go to a Kabuki performance? What traditional music or theatre do you have in your country? Do you think it's unusual for people from other countries?

QUIZATHON!

Guess the answers to these questions. Then match to the answers below.

1 How much did someone pay for the most expensive violin in the world? $_____

2 How tall is the world's biggest drum? _____ metres

3 How heavy is the world's largest bell? _____ kilos

4 How long is the world's smallest violin? _____ centimetres

5 How old is the oldest instrument found? _____ years

> 42,000   6   4.1   16,000,000   202,000

CONFIDENCE BOOST

Some people say I can't sing,
Some people say I can't dance.
That may be true but I don't care.
I love to sing and I love to dance.
Give me a chance and I won't stop,
Just don't stand too close.

LIVING IN EXTREME CONDITIONS

We humans really are a bit special – we live all over this amazing world of ours in some pretty extreme conditions. We live in some of the highest, wettest, coldest, hottest, driest parts of the planet. Next time you go out and complain that the weather's not very nice, think about people who live in or inhabit these places.

The wettest place on Earth where people live: Meghalaya State, India

How wet? Very! It has more rain a year than any other town on the planet: almost 12 metres! As an example, a 'normal' city like New York has around one metre of rain every year. In Meghalaya, the combination of heat and the rain means that nothing lasts very long. One solution they have discovered is to make bridges using living tree roots. (When it's so wet, you really need bridges.)

This bridge is 500 years old and is made of living tree roots.

The driest place on Earth where people live: Arica, Chile (although some people disagree)

Arica has less than one cm of rain every year. However, although it has less rain than anywhere else, it's not very dry. Arica sits in a valley and although it almost never rains, the air is humid. This means that a lot of fruit can grow in the area. The Atacama Desert, which is very near Arica, is one of the driest places on Earth. In some places it hasn't rained for over 500 years.

Although there's very little rain there's lots of water in the air.

Would you prefer to live somewhere that was very wet or very dry? Why? What problems do you think people have living in very dry or very wet places?

 Home mission

Ask the people at home about the places they've visited. Remember, they could be places in your country.

Find out:

1 What's the most beautiful place they've visited?
2 What's the hottest place they've visited?
3 What's the coldest place they've visited?
4 What's the busiest place they've visited?

WINDOW TO THE WORLD

How many pupils are there in your school? There are probably more pupils in your school than people who live in the Vatican, which is the world's smallest country. Not only is it the smallest country geographically (0.44 km²) but it also has the smallest population (fewer than 500 people).

Here are two other very small countries. See if you can find out how big they are and how many people live there: Monaco, Nauru.

QUIZATHON!

What do you know about the world's population? Guess the answers and then research the ones you don't know.

1 The population of the world is around 7.6 billion, which one of these is correct?

7,600,000,000	☐
7,000,600,000	☐
7,600,000	☐
7,000,600	☐

2 A baby is born somewhere in the world roughly every eight seconds. How many babies are born in an hour?

3 There are more people in China than any other country, but which country has the second biggest population?

4 Which continent has the lowest population?

CONFIDENCE BOOST

So many places to see,
So many things to do.
So many places to be,
Where am I going to?
Take your time and you will
see what's important to you.

5

BANK NOTES – MORE THAN JUST PAPER

You go to the shop, you want to buy something, you hand over a note or some coins. In exchange for the money, the shop gives you an ice-cream, or a book or whatever you want to buy. It works because we all trust the notes we use; we know they're real. Have you ever really looked at the money you use? I mean, really looked at a bank note? Most bank notes are very high-tech, they have all sorts of ways of preventing copies being made. To you and me they just feel like a piece of paper or perhaps plastic. Here are some of the features that stop notes from being copied.

In this picture you can see a window and the number ten.

Raised ink: A good way to test a note is to use your sense of touch because you can't always trust what your eyes are telling you. This is why many bank notes use a special technique on parts of the note that make the writing feel bumpy. When you move your finger across the writing you can feel the bumps.

Holograms: These are amazing pictures that are printed on the notes. When you move the note the image looks as though it is in three dimensions. Different colours appear when you move the note. That's very hard to copy.

Watermark: this is a very common feature but still quite special. When you hold up a note to the light you can see a picture as if it were inside the note.

Nowadays the watermark or hologram are printed in a little plastic window which is even harder to copy.

Take a look at some of the bank notes from your and other countries. Do they use watermarks or holograms? What pictures do they have?

WINDOW TO THE WORLD

Many countries are using fewer bank notes and coins and more things like credit cards and their phones to pay. Some people say that Sweden could be the first country to only use plastic money. Of everything that Swedes bought and sold in shops in 2016, only around 1% was paid for using notes or coins.

Do you have a piggy bank? How are you going to save money when there are no notes or coins?

QUIZATHON!

Here are some questions about money. Guess the answers and then do some research to check.

1 How many countries use the Euro? Is it 18, 19, 20, 21?

2 How many countries use the Dollar as their main currency? Is it 10, 11, 12, 13?

3 What is the currency in Japan called? The Pen, The Yen, The Sen?

4 Which are the biggest banknotes in: the US, the UK, in Euros?

5 What is the biggest banknote in your country?

6 How many different sizes of bank-notes are there in your country?

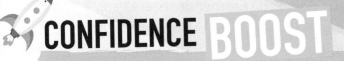

CONFIDENCE BOOST

If it's your mum's or your dad's birthday but your piggy bank is empty.
Think of things you can do that will make them happy, there's plenty.
Clean the house or wash the car,
Do the shopping but don't go far.
So, give your mum and dad a chair.
Put your coins away,
And show them that you care.

⊛ Home mission

Do you know how much these things cost? Ask everyone in your home and see who's closest. Add two very common foods in your country to the list.

A kilo of rice					
A loaf of bread					
A litre of milk					

TRAVEL GAMES

You've been stuck in traffic for three hours, and you are bored, bored, bored. What do you do? Do you put on your headphones and just look out of the window? Do you put up with being bored? Well, take off your headphones and try some of these travel games.

I Spy

This is the classic game played by families all over the English-speaking world. One person starts by saying: 'I spy with my little eye something beginning with, C.' They have to choose something you can all see. Then all the other players take turns to guess the word: 'Is it cow'? 'Is it car'? The person who guesses correctly picks the next word.

This is a good game for all ages but be warned, small children can play this game for hours.

20 questions

This game is a little bit like I Spy. Think of a thing, a person, a film. The other players ask you a maximum of 20 questions to try to guess what it is. But be careful, you can only answer 'yes' or 'no'.

I'm going to the shops

This is a memory game. The first player starts by saying: 'I'm going to the shops to buy an apple.' The next player says: 'I'm going to the shops to buy an apple and a banana.' The game continues in alphabetical order. It starts easy but then get very difficult very quickly.

Spot the red car

This is a very, very simple game, which is good, because sometimes, when you're bored, you don't want to think too much. Choose a colour or a type of car and then see how many you see in five minutes. Surprisingly enjoyable and easy to play.

Silence Game

Maybe your little brother or sister keeps asking: 'Are we there yet? How long?' Or saying: 'I need the toilet.' This game works well, but only for a few minutes. The rule is: who can keep quiet for the longest time? Your challenge is to get other players to break their silence. Try making them laugh or doing something silly.

Do you play any of these games in your country? Which other games do you play?

CONFIDENCE BOOST

Nice car, nice bike, nice shoes. It's nice to have something nice.

But it's more important to have something that works.

⭐ **Home mission**

Print or draw a simple map of your city. Put an X where your house is. Ask everyone in your house where they went and how they travelled today. Draw the routes onto the map. Who travelled the biggest distance?

QUIZATHON!

Do you think you are very active? Answer these questions to find out.

1   How many steps do you take to go from your front door to your bedroom door?
    Guess: _____
    Actual number: _____

2   How many steps are there from the school gate to your classroom door?
    Guess: _____
    Actual number: _____

3   How many stairs do you walk up on a normal day?
    Guess: _____
    Actual number: _____

4   Do you always run or walk up the stairs? _____

WINDOW TO THE WORLD

Do you live in a hilly place? Do you have to walk up hills? Have you ever tried to cycle up a hill? It's not easy, is it? Well, in Trondheim, in Norway, there is a lift for bicycles. You put your foot on the moving rail and it carries you, and your bike, up the hill. Sadly, it's the only one in the world.

Here are two other interesting ways to get around. See what you can find out about:

The elevated train in Wuppertal, Germany.

The outdoor escalator in Medellin, Colombia.

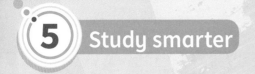

MUSCLE MEMORY

Learning a language, as you know, is not easy. Very often you feel confident until your teacher asks you a question. Suddenly, your eyes open wide, your mouth opens a little and … nothing comes out. Blank, you've forgotten absolutely everything. You feel confused and very anxious. You don't understand what happened.

Is this what you look like when your teacher asks you a question?

Part of the problem is that you need to develop what is called 'muscle memory'. When somebody throws a ball, your reaction is to catch it. You do it without thinking: this is muscle memory. This is a skill you started to learn when you were still a baby. It takes time and practice. Remember, you probably dropped the ball hundreds of times before you could catch it.

It's the same when you're learning a language. You need lots and lots of practice.

Here are some top tips:

- Talk to the mirror. The mirror will always wait for you and won't laugh at you if you make a mistake.

- Talk to yourself. The muscles in your mouth need to practise the sounds. It doesn't matter if other people think you're a bit strange, you're practising. Have a conversation, it's all good practice.

- Most importantly, repeat, repeat, repeat.

This sounds a bit strange, and you might feel a bit silly but it really will help. Choose a useful piece of language, for example: *I've eaten …*, *I've never …*, *I've always wanted …*. Think how you can finish the sentences and have a go.

WINDOW TO THE WORLD

Do you complain that you want more homework? Probably not. But if you live in Finland maybe you do. Research that was carried out a few years ago showed that many children in Finland do less than three hours of homework every week.

What do you think? Would you like less homework? Do you think homework is important?

CONFIDENCE BOOST

The top, the first, the best.
It's good to aim high.
But do you really want to be,
Better than the rest?
Isn't it better to be,
The best that you can be?

⭐ Home mission

Find out the study habits of everyone at home and complete the table.

	....	....	....
What are/ were their favourite subjects?			
How many hours of homework do/did they do every week?			
Do they have any top study tips?			
What is/was their most and least favourite subject?			

Which study tips do you think you could use?

Test your memory. Look at the pictures for 30 seconds, then close your books and write as many as you remember.

THE BEST JOB IN THE WORLD?

Do you know what job you want to do when you're older? Maybe a doctor, maybe a truck driver, maybe an architect, possibly a hairdresser, perhaps a musician? These are all very good jobs. What do they have in common? You need to train, you need experience, you need practice and you need to work hard. Have you ever thought about what the best job in the world might be?

Look at this picture. What is she doing? She's cuddling a panda – that means she must be a panda carer. Believe it or not, that's right, all she has to do is spend time with and give lots of love to baby pandas.

Do you want to apply for the job? Well, that's a little bit harder. You need to be at least 22 years old (sorry you have to wait a few years) and know a little about pandas.

Do you know how many people applied for this job? No one's sure but somewhere around 100,000 people. We clearly like pandas! Is this the best job in the world?

Do you think you would like this job? Why or why not? Do you think this is a real job? Is it hard work?

WINDOW TO THE WORLD

Do you ever order pizza online or on the phone? The pizza delivery person usually arrives by bike or by car but not if you stay at Jules Undersea Lodge in Florida. Here, if you order pizza it will be delivered to you by an underwater pizza delivery person. Don't worry, the pizza won't get wet.

Would you like to stay in an underwater hotel? Why or why not?

Would you like to be an underwater pizza delivery person?

QUIZATHON!

Take a look at the jobs and the list of characteristics. What do you think you need for each job? There's no right or wrong but make sure you can explain your answer.

Job	Characteristics
Doctor	hard-working
	good with people
Engineer	enjoy studying
	enjoy puzzles
Nurse	a good listener
	kind
Teacher	patient
	good at drawing
Architect	organised
	good memory

Which characteristics do you have?

🚀 CONFIDENCE BOOST

You still have plenty of time to think about the jobs you want to do.
Architect, cleaner, scientist or sailor, it's totally up to you.

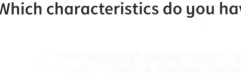

Home mission

Talk to the people at home. Find out how many jobs they've done and whether or not they liked them.

Name	List of jobs	Did they like them? Why/Why not?

Which was their favourite job? Do you want to do the same job?

13

THE HELPFUL BURGLAR

There are many headlines about criminals who make silly mistakes during their crimes. For example, there are lots of stories about thieves who post selfies in the middle of a crime. This gives the police all the information they need to catch the criminal.

What is more unusual is to have a helpful burglar. Normally a burglar breaks into your house to steal things. But one burglar in England broke in and did the washing up and tidied up the house. The owners of the house returned home after their holiday. When they opened the door, they discovered a man asleep in one of their beds. He hadn't done any damage, he hadn't stolen anything, in fact he'd tidied up the house. He'd also done some shopping, made dinner, had a bath and washed some clothes.

The couple didn't wake up the man, instead they called the police. When the police arrived the man was still fast asleep. Reports claim the man thought that nobody lived in the house and because he needed somewhere to sleep he broke into the property.

The couple who discovered the thief were shocked but they weren't scared. They were happy he hadn't stolen anything.

CONFIDENCE BOOST

It's easy to make mistakes
It's what we all do.
It's hard to say sorry.
Because that's up to you.

WINDOW TO THE WORLD

Iceland is a large, beautiful island in the Norwegian Sea. Just over 330,000 people live there. It's a very peaceful place and it also has one of the lowest prison populations in the world – around 130 people. Many people live in villages and small towns, which means neighbours help each other a lot more than in a big city.

How do you help your neighbours?
How do your neighbours help you?

QUIZATHON!

Can you solve this puzzle? How does John know that Lucy is lying?

John: Is that my £5?

Lucy: No, this is mine. I found it between pages 67 and 68 of my book.

John: You're lying – I can prove it.

Home mission

Discuss these crimes with your family. Can you think of an unusual punishment for each one?

1   Someone who breaks into houses.
2   Someone who steals people's identities.
3   Someone who cheats in exams.
4   Someone who drives too fast.

THE FUTURE OF FOOD

The world's population is growing fast. At the moment there are around seven billion people in the world, that's a seven + nine zeros. In the next fifty years, the population is likely to grow up to 10,000,000,000. Sadly, not everyone has enough to eat but this kind of population growth means we all need to think differently about food. Here are some ideas to think about.

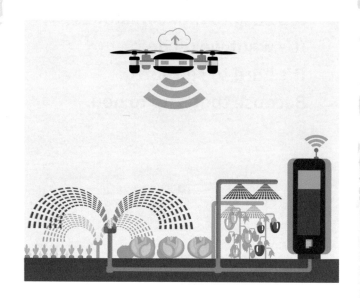

Growing food in the right places

One part of the problem is getting all those tasty vegetables from the farm to the people that need it. Think about it, one cucumber is quite heavy so 100 cucumbers are very heavy. They all need to be packed into lorries and driven hundreds of miles. But now more and more food is being grown in the cities.

Growing food vertically

The main problem in cities is that there's no space and land is very expensive. This means that very soon you might see vertical farms. Instead of growing horizontally you grow upwards, almost like flats in a building.

Aqua culture

For hundreds of years farmers have grown certain foods together, what one plant doesn't need the other uses for energy. This is what happens in aquaponics. The fish make the water dirty but this dirty water is full of food that helps the plants grow. The plants take the food and make the water cleaner.

Meat from a test tube

This last one might sound a little strange: meat, not from an animal but from a laboratory. Does that mean that vegetarians could eat this meat? Would you eat meat from a test tube?

Which do you think is the best idea? Why?

WINDOW TO THE WORLD

What's more important, for the food to look good or for it to taste nice? Or perhaps it's a bit of both? There is a restaurant in Paris with branches globally (London, Melbourne and Auckland) where you eat your food in complete darkness – you can't see anything. The waiters are all blind so they have no problem finding you or your table. Would you like to visit this restaurant? Why or why not?

QUIZATHON!

Can you think of a food for every letter of the alphabet? Some letters are very difficult!

A = apple, b = banana ...

CONFIDENCE BOOST

You can't say you don't like it,
Until you've tried it
Try it once, try it twice, try it three times.
Just a little bit.
You know you might like it,
After you've tried it.
Tried it once,
tried it twice,
tried it three times.

⭐ Home mission

Find out what the people at home think about the following ideas:

1 Could you live as a vegetarian? Why or why not? (If you are a vegetarian: do you think you could go back to eating meat? Why or why not?)
2 Would you eat meat that is grown in a laboratory? Why or why not?
3 What's the most amazing meal you've ever had?
4 What's the most disappointing meal you've ever had?

IT'S RAINING FROGS AND ALLIGATORS?

We all know what rain is, don't we? Water vapour that condenses, forms a cloud and then falls from the sky. And, yes, when it rains this is what happens … usually. However, there have been reports of some very strange things falling from the sky instead of rain. Here are some examples.

Falling Frogs

One day in 1981, in a city in Southern Greece, people went out into the streets to find thousands of small frogs falling from the sky. Scientists believe they were picked up in a strong wind and carried all the way to Greece. However, these frogs lived in North Africa and so were carried in the clouds for hundreds of miles.

Solid squid

Back in 1997 a Korean fisherman was out at sea when suddenly something fell out of the sky and hit him on the head. Believe it or not it was a frozen squid.

Ali the Alligator

A frog is quite small. It's easy to see how it could be picked up in a storm and then dropped during a shower, but an alligator? Yes, in 1843 in the Southern United States, residents of Charleston, left their houses after a storm and came face to face with an alligator that was half a metre long. The local newspaper reported that it was looking a bit confused but well.

You may not have seen anything like this, but what's the biggest storm you've seen? Were you scared?

⊛ Home mission

Talk to the people at home. Tell them they have three wishes for now and the future. Write them here.

Ask them about: travel and work. You could also ask them what wishes they have for your future.

	Wish 1	Wish 2	Wish 3
Name			
Name			
Name			
Name			

WINDOW TO THE WORLD

How cold is cold? If you live anywhere near Yakutsk in Eastern Russia cold means -50°C – that's minus 50 degrees Celsius. In these temperatures everything freezes. If you wear glasses you have to be careful when you take them off as they could pull off some skin. What is perhaps most amazing is that in these temperatures, schools are still open and workers on building sites are still building houses.

What does 'cold' mean in your city?

Do you have heating in your home?

Do you prefer it to be too hot or too cold?

No need for freezers at the market in Yakutsk.

QUIZATHON!

Guess the answers and then check.

1 **What's the freezing point of water?** -2°C / 0°C / 2°C

2 **What's the freezing point of salt water?** -2°C / 0°C / 2°C

3 **What's the boiling point of water?** 100°C / 200°C / 80°C

4 **If you are on the top of a mountain is the boiling point higher or lower?**

5 **Can it snow when the temperature is above 0°C?**

6 **What's the hottest temperature ever recorded?** 48°C / 58°C / 68°C

7 **What's the coldest temperature ever recorded?** -89°C / -99°C / -109°C

8 **What's the normal temperature of the human body?**

9 **What's the name of the metal used in thermometers? Why is it special?**

CONFIDENCE BOOST

It's good to have wishes and dream about what to do.
But there's only one way to make them come true.
Don't wait for the wish to come to you.
Work hard and make it come to you.

Writing a biography using facts

1 **Discuss the questions with a partner.**

- Who's your favorite singer?
- What is he or she most famous for?

2 **Read the biography of Dua Lipa. Then answer the questions.**

DUA LIPA

Dua Lipa is an English singer who was born in London in 1995. Her parents are from Albania. Her father is also a singer. Dua is famous for singing and writing her own songs, which are a mix of hip-hop and pop. Her videos are also very popular.

Dua loved singing, but when she was eleven, her teacher didn't think she was a good singer and wouldn't let her join the school's singing group. So she continued to practise, and later went to the Sylvia Young Theatre School, where other famous actors and singers, including Leona Lewis and Rita Ora, also studied.

When she was fifteen years old, she began posting videos on YouTube of her singing songs by other pop singers. In 2015, her first song, 'New Love', was a big success and was in the top ten in many European countries, Australia, and New Zealand. Her success continued, and in 2017 she had

four songs in the top 10 in the UK. In 2018, she won two awards at the Brit Awards.

Although she is best known for her songs and videos, she's also involved in charity and helps to raise money for different charity organisations.

1 Where was Dua Lipa's father born? _____

2 What happened when she was eleven years old? _____

3 What does she have in common with Leona Lewis and Rita Ora? _____

4 What happened in 2017? _____

5 Apart from music, what else does she do? _____

Differences between fact and opinion

Use facts, not opinions in biographies. You can prove a fact: *In 2018, Dua Lipa won two awards.*

You can't prove an opinion: *Dua Lipa is one of the best singers in Europe.* Opinions often use words like *the best, worse than, I think.*

3 **Read the tip.** Then choose the two facts which you could include in the Dua Lipa biography.

a   She has a sister and a brother.

b   I think her teacher probably regrets that decision now.

c   She used to work in a restaurant.

d   Her best song of 2017 was 'Blow your Mind'.

4 **Read the tip.** Then choose the correct plural.

Plural of nouns ending in *o*

For nouns that end in vowel + *o*, we usually add *s* = *videos*

For nouns that end in consonant + *o*, we either add *s* = *photos* OR *es* = *heroes*

When you learn a word that ends in *o*, learn the plural form!

1   radios / radioes

2   pianos / pianoes

3   kilos / kiloes

5 **Think about a singer or dancer. Complete the spider diagram.**

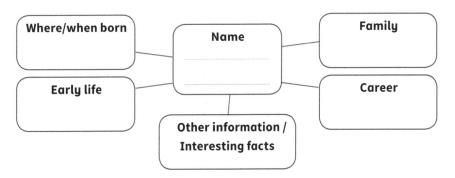

Where/when born — Name — Family

Early life — Name — Career

Name — Other information / Interesting facts

6 **Use your notes to write a biography about your singer or dancer in your notebook.**

7 **Check your partner's biography.**

● Has your partner included the important facts in a good order?

● Check that your partner has given facts and not opinions.

● Check the spelling. Focus on words that end in 'o'.

Writing a magazine article with headings

1 Imagine you're moving to another country tomorrow. How do you feel?

2 Read the article. Are the sentences true or false?

1 _____

2 _____

When I was ten, my dad got a new job here in Kenya. I wasn't very happy at first, but I didn't have a choice. He moved here at the beginning of the summer holidays to find us a new house, and we followed a month later.

3 _____

When we arrived at Mombasa airport, the first thing I noticed was the heat. It was 30 degrees in September! My dad hired a car and he took us to our new huge house by the beach.

4 _____

We didn't go to school for a few weeks. While Dad was at work, I spent time with my mum and sister getting to know the area. We spent a lot of time on the beach and tried lots of new food from the local restaurants.

5 _____

My sister is older than me, so she went to an international secondary school in the city. I went to the local village school. It was difficult at the beginning because the children spoke Kiswahili at break times. In England, maths was my favourite subject, but here in Kenya, I was no longer the best student. But gradually, after a lot of hard work, I'm doing better at school. I've made lots of friends and I'm learning a new language!

Lisa

Mark the sentences True or False.

1 Lisa flew to Kenya with her mum, dad and sister. ___

2 It was very hot on the day she arrived in Kenya. ___

3 Her dad bought a new car when he arrived in Kenya. ___

4 Lisa ate lots of Kenyan food when she arrived. ___

5 Lisa and her sister went to the same school. ___

6 Lisa can speak a little Kiswahili. ___

3 **Read the tip. Then put the heading and subheadings in the correct place.**

a   A shock to the senses on arrival

b   Bad news for Lisa

c   British family swaps rainy UK for sunny Kenya!

d   How life has changed

e   Time together in our new home

4 **Read the tip. Then circle the four words that follow the rule.**

wrote   love   lake   place   have   wife

5 **Imagine you have moved to another country. Complete the notes.**

where: _____

when: _____

why: _____

problems: _____

what it's like now: _____

6 **Use your notes to write a magazine article about moving to another country in your notebook.**

7 **Check your partner's article.**

●   Has your partner included the important details and in a logical order?

●   Check that your partner has included short, interesting headings.

●   Check the spelling. Focus on words with vowel + consonant + vowel.

Writing a story with paragraphs

1 **Do you like buying second-hand items?** Why / why not?

2 **Read the story.** Then answer the questions.

My granny Felicity volunteers in a charity shop and really enjoys it. She has lots of friends there and because she's so talkative, she loves chatting with the customers. It's nice for her to do something that raises money for other people, too. She always has something interesting to tell us about her day, but then last week, something amazing happened!

She was putting the prices on the second-hand books: 50p for one book, three for £1 as usual. Then she picked up a book that was a bit damaged. It was about stamps. She thought, 'who wants a book about stamps?' and put it by the bin and forgot about it.

At the end of a very busy day, she was picking up the rubbish to take outside when **she looked at the book again**. It suddenly seemed familiar. She opened it and recognised her grandfather's handwriting. So it wasn't worth much, but actually, to her it was worth more than a thousand books!

When she came home, **she phoned the whole family and we went to see it**. And do you know what the most interesting thing is? My grandma's shop isn't in the town her grandfather lived in. We don't know how it got there, but we're very pleased it did!

1 What is Felicity like?

2 How much do books at the charity shop usually cost?

3 Why didn't Felicity look closely at the stamp book?

4 Who did the book belong to and how did Felicity know?

5 Is Felicity going to sell the book?

6 Why is it strange that the book was in Felicity's shop?

Paragraphs
When writing a story, write a new paragraph for each event.

The first sentence of each paragraph, or the topic sentence, should give an idea about what the new event is. Look at the sentence parts in bold for examples.

3 **Read the tip. Then choose the best topic sentence.**

1 His favourite was cheese, tomato, ham and olives.

2 My brother booked a trip to Italy for after his final exams.

3 He thought they were really friendly and spent a lot of time with them.

4 Unfortunately, the shop didn't have one in his size.

4 **Read the tip. Then choose the correct spelling.**

SPELLING TIP!
Compound nouns
In English we can join two words together to make new words.

Sometimes this is just one word (*grandfather*) or two words (*charity shop*). It's a good idea to check in a dictionary.

1 football / foot ball

2 postoffice / post office

3 bathroom / bath room

4 breakfast / break fast

5 swimmingpool / swimming pool

5 **Imagine you buy something unusual in a shop. What happens? Complete the notes.**

Paragraph 1: Introduction

Paragraph 2: What happened first?

Paragraph 3: What happened next?

Paragraph 4: What happened at the end?

6 **Use your notes to write a story about something unusual you bought in a shop in your notebook.**

7 **Check your partner's story.**

● Has your partner included any interesting details?

● Check that your partner has written clear paragraphs in a logical order.

● Check the spelling. Focus on compound nouns.

Writing a letter giving important information

1 **Choose one of your school subjects.** Think of a good place to go for a school trip. Why is it a good choice?

2 **Read the letter.** Find the numbers, times or dates.

Dear Parents,

This year, class 3 is studying French artists so we have decided to arrange a five-day trip to Paris. This is an excellent opportunity for our students and we hope as many as possible can attend.

We will be flying from London on Friday 17th March and returning on Tuesday 21st March. We will be staying with local families so that students can practise their French too. There will be a good mix of fun and educational activities: we'll be visiting museums, art galleries and tourist attractions, but there will be enough time too for shopping and relaxing in the evenings. Tickets have been reserved for a show on the last evening.

Your son or daughter will need to be at school at 5 a.m. on Friday as the bus to the airport leaves at 5.50. The cost is £325 each plus spending money. There isn't much space on the coach, so please keep luggage to a minimum. Everyone will need to look after their own passports.

Please complete the one-page form if you would like your son or daughter to attend.

Best wishes,

Mrs Pearce (Art teacher)

1   cost: _____
2   date of departure: _____
3   time coach leaves: _____

4   date of return: _____
5   name of class: _____
6   length of trip: _____

3   **Read the tip. Then work with a partner. Cross out the information which isn't needed. Can you delete 25 words?**

The new American horror film is at 7.10 on Saturday at the cinema in the shopping centre. There are lots of cafes nearby. It's £5.20 for adults, but as we're students, it costs £4.20. Let's meet at 7.00. My mum's taking me, so I'll see you there!

4   **Read the tip. Then use the words to write four expressions. There is more than one possible answer.**

one	two	three	four
door	hour	minute	page
break	movie	form	car

1 _____   2 _____   3 _____   4 _____

5   **Make notes for a letter.**

Imagine you're the president of a club at your school. You and a teacher have arranged a trip for the students. Your teacher has asked you to write a letter to the parents. Make notes about the important information.

1   name of club: _____
2   where the club will go: _____
3   length of trip: _____

4   cost: _____
5   dates for leaving and returning: _____
6   time coach leaves: _____

6   **Use your notes to write a letter in your notebook.**

7   **Check your partner's letter.**

● Has your partner included the important details?

● Check that your partner has not included anything that is not needed.

● Check the spelling. Focus on compound adjectives with numbers.

Writing a report about a survey

1 **Look at the bar charts.** Then answer the questions.

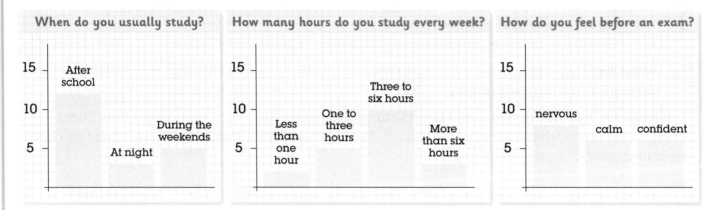

| When do you usually study? | How many hours do you study every week? | How do you feel before an exam? |

1 When do the fewest number of students study? _____

2 How many hours a week do most students spend studying? _____

3 How many students feel nervous before an exam? _____

2 **Read the report.** Then answer the questions.

This is a report about how students in my class study. I asked them to answer three questions about their study habits and how they feel about exams.

First, I wanted to know when they liked to study. The results were clear: more students prefer to study after school than at night or at weekends. This means that most students have free time at the weekends to relax.

Then, I asked how much time they spent studying. The most popular answer was three to six hours. The least popular answer was less than one hour. This information tells us that most of the students in my class work hard.

Finally, I asked about their feelings before an exam. Two more people said nervous than calm or confident, but two out of twenty isn't many.

In conclusion, I think most people in my class have good study habits and a good attitude to exams. We work hard, but we also have enough time to relax.

1 Why did the writer of the report ask students questions?

2 What do we know about what students do at the weekends?

3 How do we know that students in the class are hard-working?

4 What were the three options for question 3?

5 Is the writer positive or negative about the students in his class?

3 **Read the tip.** Match the figures.

1	half	a	most
2	nine out of ten	b	few
3	two in fifty	c	50 percent

4 **Read the tip.** Then make the *-ing* form of the verbs.

1	do	3	dance	5	go	7	worry
2	hope	4	fix	6	cry	8	make

5 **Look at the bar charts about taking exams.** Make notes. Remember to say what the information tells you.

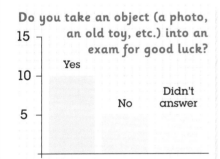
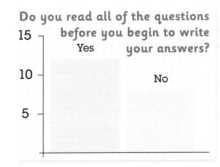
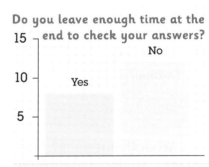

6 **Use your notes to write a report about the survey in your notebook.**

7 **Check your partner's report.**

- Has your partner included an introduction, sentences about each question and a conclusion?
- Check that your partner has talked about the numbers in a variety of ways and has analysed the results.
- Check the spelling. Focus on verbs with the *-ing* form.

Writing a formal application letter with an introduction and a conclusion

1 **What jobs can people your age do?**

2 **Read the advert and the letter and answer the questions.**

Bournemouth Pet Shelter

Dog Walker wanted: to walk, brush, feed and water dogs, wash out food and water bowls. Saturdays and some school holidays. Write to Tina Thomas, 16 Stour Drive, Bournemouth

16 Stour Drive
Bournemouth
8th May
Dear Mrs Thomas,

I'm writing to you about the dog walker job that I saw an advert for at the pet shelter. I would like to apply for the job, and I think I can really help the animals at your pet shelter.

I'm 12 years old and I'm in Year 7. I am a good student. I work hard and I'm always on time. I want to be an animal doctor when I grow up.

I have a dog and a cat at home. So, I'm very good at taking care of pets. I know how to brush a dog without pulling any fur and how to talk to a dog so that it feels calm. I can walk very big dogs easily. I can even help your cats if you need it.

I can work on Saturdays and in school holidays too. I would like to work for the pet shelter to help pets. I hope to hear from you soon. Thank you for your time.

Yours sincerely,

Hannah Jones

1 What things does a dog walker do?

2 Can someone who goes to school apply? How do you know?

3 Where did Hannah see the advert?

4 What does she want to do in the future?

5 What experience does she have?

6 Do you think she'll get the job? Why? / Why not?

3 **Read the tip.** Which sentences would Hannah NOT write in a formal letter of application?

1 My mum said you want someone to walk dogs.

2 I can work most Saturdays if you want, but I see my cousins some weekends.

3 I've practised cutting my dog's nails and know how to do it safely.

4 **Read the tip.** Then circle the four adjectives with a silent *l*.

would   self   half   help   salmon   could

5 **Look at the advert below.** Why would you be good for the job? Make notes.

> **Newspaper carrier needed**
> **John's Newspapers, Apply in person at Newspaper office**
> **One hour before school Monday–Friday AND school holidays**
> **Start 7 am. Own bike needed**

Reason 1: _____

Reason 2: _____

Reason 3: _____

6 **Use your notes to write a formal letter of application for the job in Activity 5 in your notebook.**

7 **Check your partner's letter.**

- Has your partner included a good introduction and conclusion?

- Check that your partner has answered all the points in the advert.

- Check the spelling. Focus on words with the letter 'l'.

Creating a play using stage directions and direct speech

1 **Think of a play you've watched or read.** What was it about?

2 **Read the play.** Are the sentences true or false?

[Anna and Sophie are in a maths class. They're whispering.]

Anna   What are you doing tonight, Sophie?
Sophie   Oh, nothing much. I might watch a film.

[Their teacher is at the board talking to the class.]

Mrs Smith   And then if you add two, then you get …

[Anna whispers again.]

Anna   Do you understand what she's saying?
Sophie   Not really. You're talking, and I'm trying to listen!
Anna   Oh, sorry.

[ten minutes later]

Mrs Smith   Right. Leave your books on the table. See you tomorrow!
All   See you tomorrow, Mrs Smith.

[After lunch, in English class. Mr Talbot, the headteacher, comes in.]

Mr Talbot   I'm sorry, Mrs James. Could Anna come with me, please?

[Sophie and Anna whisper again.]

Sophie   What have you done?
Anna   I have no idea!

[At the head teacher's office.]

Mr Talbot   Anna, this is serious. Do you have anything to say?
Anna   Um, I don't know what I did wrong! What did I do?
Mr Talbot   What were you doing between 11 and 12 this morning?
Anna   I was in maths class.
Mr Talbot   Do you like maths?
Anna   Not really. It's very difficult.
Mr Talbot   Is that why you drew on the desk? Were you bored?
Anna   Oh, I'm so sorry! But it isn't a permanent pen! Look, I'll write my name on this table …
Mr Talbot   Anna, you're in enough trouble already.
Anna   Look! A n n a. Now I use some water and look – it's gone!
Mr Talbot   (embarrassed) Right, um, OK, well go back to your room and I'll speak to Mrs Smith. You're at school to learn, Anna. I don't want to see you here again!

---

1   Sophie has plans for tonight. _____
2   Anna is interrupting Sophie. _____
3   Anna and Sophie give their books to the teacher. _____
4   Mr Talbot is the English teacher. _____
5   Anna asks Mr Talbot a question. _____
6   Anna is guilty of a crime. _____

3   **Read the tip.** Then write the reported speech in direct speech and write a stage direction.

He told me to show him my pen.

4   **Read the tip.** Then complete the words.

Complete the words with *f, ph,* or *gh*.

1   _oto

2   cou_

3   _antasy

4   lau_

5   _antastic

6   ele_ant

5   **Imagine a story about someone who did something wrong in school.** Complete the spider diagram.

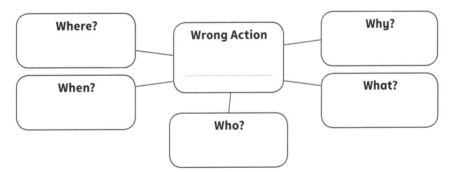

6   **Use your notes to write a play.**

7   **Check your partner's play.**

●   Has your partner included enough information about what happens?

●   Check that your partner has added stage directions and used direct speech.

●   Check the spelling. Focus on words with *f, ph* or *gh*.

8 Fantastic flavours

Writing a food blog to persuade others

1 **Think of a traditional dish from your country.** What could you do to encourage someone from another country to try it?

2 **Read the blog.** Then answer the questions.

	Profile	Photos	Share	Friends	

Hello food fans! As you know I usually blog about my favourite new restaurants and unusual dishes I've tried. But today I want to tell you about a brilliant idea I saw online! It's 'miniature food' and it was created by Turkish couple, Burcu Celenoglu Aydin and her husband, Anil. They have a tiny frying pan and tiny knives, but they haven't got a tiny fridge. They try to make their Turkish dishes taste as good as normal-sized dishes. They can do starters, main courses, and desserts. It takes longer to make the miniature food because it's difficult, but the results are amazing. Anil takes the photos himself, too.

So I've got a great idea. Why don't we all try to make a miniature dish from our countries and put them online? Here's a photo of my first try at making a mini-breakfast. Doesn't it look amazing? It was delicious! I would love to see your dishes!

♡ LIKE   COMMENT

Jessie

---

1 What does Jessie usually blog about? _____

2 What did Bercu and Anil Aydin create? _____

3 What do they use? _____

4 Does it take more or less time to make than ordinary food? _____

5 Who takes the photos? _____

6 What does Jessie want you to do? _____

Techniques to persuade others

When writing a blog, it's a good idea to sound positive and enthusiastic.

Use expressions like 'Why don't we …', 'I've got a great idea', and rhetorical questions 'Doesn't it look amazing?' to encourage other people to do things.

3 **Read the tip.** Then write an enthusiastic sentence for the suggestions.

go to the cinema   tidy your room   do your homework   go to London

_____

_____

4 **Read the tip.** Then complete the words with *ce* or *ge*.
One word can have two endings.

SPELLING TIP! *ce / ge*

We add an *e* after *c* to make it sound like /s/, and an *e* after *g* to make it sound like /j/.

1 dan _____   3 lar _____   5 pea _____
2 chan _____   4 senten _____

5 **Imagine you have a food blog.** Think of a type of food you want people to try.
Why should they try it? How would you get them to try it? Make notes.

_____

_____

_____

6 **Use your notes to write a blog.**

7 **Check your partner's blog.**

● Has your partner included enough details?

● Check that your partner has used techniques to persuade.

● Check the spelling. Focus on words with *ce* and *ge*.

Writing a product review presenting reasons and opinions

1 **Discuss with a partner.** How do you choose what type of shoes or clothes to buy?

2 **Read the product review.** Then number the ideas from the review in the correct order.

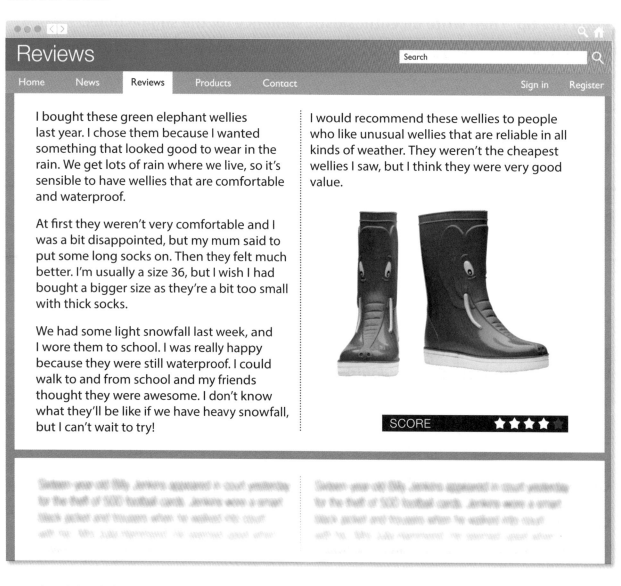

Reviews

| Home | News | Reviews | Products | Contact | | Sign in | Register |

I bought these green elephant wellies last year. I chose them because I wanted something that looked good to wear in the rain. We get lots of rain where we live, so it's sensible to have wellies that are comfortable and waterproof.

At first they weren't very comfortable and I was a bit disappointed, but my mum said to put some long socks on. Then they felt much better. I'm usually a size 36, but I wish I had bought a bigger size as they're a bit too small with thick socks.

We had some light snowfall last week, and I wore them to school. I was really happy because they were still waterproof. I could walk to and from school and my friends thought they were awesome. I don't know what they'll be like if we have heavy snowfall, but I can't wait to try!

I would recommend these wellies to people who like unusual wellies that are reliable in all kinds of weather. They weren't the cheapest wellies I saw, but I think they were very good value.

SCORE ★★★★☆

___ Friends' opinions

___ Size

___ What they look like

___ Reason for choice

___ Price

___ Who they're good for

> **WRITING TIP!** **Presenting reasons and opinions**
>
> When writing a product review, remember to give reasons for your opinions. Try to persuade people to buy or not to buy your product.
>
> **Example**
>
> *This umbrella is terrible because when it was windy, it broke! Don't buy it.* ✓
>
> *This umbrella is terrible. Don't buy it.* ✗

3 **Read the tip.** Then make the sentence better.

Buy this raincoat. _____

4 **Read the tip.** Then choose the correct spelling.

> **SPELLING TIP!** *ible / able*
>
> We can add *-ible* or *-able* to words to make adjectives. If a word is a whole word, we can usually add *-able* (*comfort – comfortable*), or we can remove the *e* (*value – valuable*). If the word isn't a whole word on its own, we add *-ible* (*poss – possible*). There are always exceptions (*sense – sensible*), so remember to check in your dictionary.

1 invisable/invisible
2 possable/possible

3 predictable/ible
4 responsable/responsible

5 **Imagine you bought one of the following items.** Complete the spider diagram.

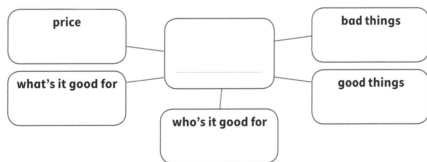

price

what's it good for

bad things

good things

who's it good for

6 **Use your notes to write a product review.**

7 **Check your partner's product review.**

- Has your partner included enough information?
- Check that your partner has said why the product is good or not and has given examples and arguments.
- Check the spelling. Focus on words with *ible / able* endings.